Racism

ISSUES
(formerly Issues for the Nineties)

Volume 6

Editor

Craig Donnellan

Independence
Educational Publishers
Cambridge

First published by Independence
PO Box 295
Cambridge CB1 3XP
England

British Library Cataloguing in Publication Data
Racism – (Issues Series)
I. Donnellan, Craig II. Series
305.8

ISBN 1 86168 091 0

Printed in Great Britain
The Burlington Press
Cambridge

Typeset by
Claire Boyd

Cover
The illustration on the front cover is by
Pumpkin House.

CONTENTS

Chapter One: Tackling Racism

Chapter Two: Racism at Work

Chapter Three: Racism in Football

Introduction

Racism is the sixth volume in the series: **Issues**. The aim of this series is to offer up-to-date information about important issues in our world.

Racism looks at the issues of racism in the community, at work and in sport.

The information comes from a wide variety of sources and includes:
Government reports and statistics
Newspaper reports and features
Magazine articles and surveys
Literature from lobby groups
and charitable organisations.

It is hoped that, as you read about the many aspects of the issues explored in this book, you will critically evaluate the information presented. It is important that you decide whether you are being presented with facts or opinions. Does the writer give a biased or an unbiased report? If an opinion is being expressed, do you agree with the writer?

Racism offers a useful starting-point for those who need convenient access to information about the many issues involved. However, it is only a starting-point. At the back of the book is a list of organisations which you may want to contact for further information.

*****

Racial attacks and harassment

What are they?

If someone abuses or threatens you or damages your property because of your colour, race, nationality or ethnic origin that is racial harassment. If someone uses any kind of physical violence against you because of your colour, race, nationality or ethnic origin that is a racial attack.

Any of the following incidents are classified as a racial attack or harassment:

- Personal attacks of any kind
- Written or verbal threats or insults
- Damage to property
- Graffiti.

There are some kinds of harassment that are dealt with separately:

- It is a crime to use threatening, abusive or insulting words or behaviour with the intention of stirring up racial hatred or where racial hatred might happen (Public Order Act 1986).
- It is a crime to use threatening, abusive or insulting behaviour when someone who will be distressed by it can see or hear it (Public Order Act 1986).
- Racial chanting or abuse at football grounds is a criminal offence (The Football Offences Act 1991).
- The Criminal Justice and Public Order Act 1994 introduced a new offence, called 'harassment with intent'. This offence carries a maximum sentence of six months' imprisonment and/or a £5,000 fine. To prove 'harassment with intent' it is necessary to show an intent to harass, alarm or distress someone and, in all cases, for the victim to give evidence.

The sorts of racial harassment cases in which the police are most likely to initiate the prosecution process are:

- Acts intended or likely to stir up racial hatred (including the display and distribution of written material).
- Cases of assault, even those which appear to be minor, so long as the victim is prepared to give evidence that some harm resulted. Pain, injury or even psychological harm such as hysterical or nervous condition is enough in these cases.
- Threatening, abusive or insulting words or behaviour which is likely to cause alarm, harassment or distress to another.
- Damage to property such as broken windows, paint daubed on doors or walls, excrement pushed through letterboxes etc.

Such acts are totally unacceptable and criminal offences.

What you should do if you are attacked or harassed

1. If you are suspicious about anyone call the police by dialling 999.

2. If you are being attacked and need immediate help call the police by dialling 999.

3. Report the attack or abuse to the police as soon as possible. Keep a record of the name of the police officer, the date and the time you reported it. Tell the police that you believe it was a racial attack, and ask them to record it as such.

4. Write down exactly what happened including details such as: the time, the place, description of attackers, the words they used, what they did, the injuries you received, who you contacted for help etc.

5. Try to get the names and addresses of any witnesses, and encourage them to write down everything they saw.

6. If you, or anyone else, is injured go to a doctor or a hospital and get them to write down the details of the injuries.

7. If possible, take photographs of the injuries.

8. Leave any evidence untouched and show it to the police.

SIMON KNEEBONE

9. Contact other organisations that can help such as a Racial Equality Council or Citizens' Advice Bureau. They will be able to advise you about where to go for help and what you can do.

What you can do at home

Incidents at home can take many ugly forms – from rubbish left on doorsteps or put through letterboxes, an unpleasant telephone call, graffiti, arson or a criminal assault.

Being aware of the dangers and taking a few sensible precautions can make all the difference.

Simple steps

- Fit a door chain and viewer and use them at all times. Check that your outside lighting lets you identify all callers.
- Even though rubbish and other filth is extremely unpleasant, and smashed glass is dangerous, try not to clean it up until the police have arrived. The most tiny clue sometimes helps.
- On returning home late at night, have your house keys ready to let yourself in quickly.
- If you are harassed on the telephone by persistent, unpleasant callers inform the operator and the police.

What you can do on the streets

Everyone has the right to go about their normal lives as they please.

Racial harassment of all kinds from verbal abuse to violent attacks on people stops this freedom. The following simple precautions can be taken to reduce the risks.

Simple Steps

- Be on your guard.
- Never walk home alone at night, unless you have no choice.
- Never take short cuts.
- Keep to busy, well-lit roads as far as possible.
- Always walk facing on-coming traffic.
- If you think you are being followed, cross the road and keep walking.
- If you continue to be followed, make for a busy area or well-lit house to ask for help. If you do

get attacked, shout or scream as loudly as you can, it might frighten your attacker(s) and attract help.

- Try not to let your attacker grab both your hands at the same time. If you're actually attacked fight back using anything to hand, such as an umbrella or a handbag. People under attack have to be prepared to defend themselves with reasonable force and with anything that is normally used, like umbrellas or car keys. One item you might find useful is a personal alarm. Carry it ready for use. It may be effective in deterring a would-be attacker. What the law does NOT allow is carrying anything which can be described as an offensive weapon e.g. knives, toxic sprays.

medidas si aparece

What you can do at school

Racial harassment occurs in schools. Badges with offensive slogans, verbal abuse, bullying and attacks are all common methods of inciting racial hatred among fellow students. On another level, racism can come from those adults who allow racial prejudice to affect their behaviour, or allow racial incidents to develop.

Active steps

- If the incident involves other children in the school, report it to the teacher or headteacher.
- Incidents of racial harassment by a particular child may be reported to the police. Incidents may be taken up with the local education authority.

What you can do at work

The Race Relations Act 1976 makes it unlawful to discriminate on racial grounds against a person directly or indirectly, in the field of employment. Intimidation by supervisors, failure by management to respond to complaints of harassment by colleagues, inequality in working conditions, unfair allocation of jobs and segregation – these would be examples of how a person is treated less favourably than others. Such behaviour is against the law. Complaints must be formally made within three months to an Industrial Tribunal.

In passing the Race Relations Act, Parliament empowered the Commission for Racial Equality to draw up a Code of Practice for Employment. The Code does not have the force of law but, if Industrial Tribunals consider any of its provisions relevant to a case before them, they must take such provisions into account. Also, individuals taking complaints of racial discrimination can call on the recommendations in support of their case.

If you run your own business, such as a shop, then harassment can also take the form of assault, vandalism, graffiti or slogan daubing on your premises. However, this is not normally covered by the Race Relations Act and is a criminal matter.

Simple steps

- Find out about the law relating to employment and racism.
- Report any incident which happens at your place of work to your employer, your union or works representative, and keep a note of your conversation.
- If you run your own business, consult with the local police Crime Prevention Officer (a police officer whose job it is to help and advise you) for free, expert advice on security.

• The above is an extract from the BLINK (Black Information Link) web site which can be found at http://www.blink.org.uk which is funded and run by The 1990 Trust.

What is racism?

Information from the Commission for Racial Equality (CRE)

Racism is the belief that people from some races are innately inferior to others, because of things like the colour of their skin, their ethnic origin, or the country that they come from. Prejudice is knowing next to nothing about people but prejudging them anyway on the basis of stereotypes.

Racial discrimination

Racial discrimination occurs when someone is treated less favourably because of their skin colour, or their racial, national or ethnic origin. Discrimination occurs because of what someone does, not what they think.

Racial discrimination includes racial abuse and harassment and is against the law.

Racism can make it harder for people to get jobs, or take away people's jobs; it can mean they have poorer housing, or that they leave school or college with fewer qualifications; it can result in violent attacks, or it can lead to harsh treatment by the police or other authorities.

How much discrimination is there?

Most of the racial discrimination that takes place in Britain today is based on 'colour', and is directed against 'visible' minorities – for example, people of Asian, African, Caribbean and Chinese descent. But all 'racial' groups (including white people) are equally protected by the Act, and the CRE can help people from any ethnic background or nationality to obtain legal redress. For example Irish people, Gypsies, Greek-Cypriots, Moroccans, Jews, and people of Serbian origin have all received help from the CRE.

It is sometimes said that claims of racial discrimination are exaggerated, and that organisations like the CRE only make matters worse. The fact is that, while life has improved in many ways for ethnic minorities in Britain since the early 1950s, racial discrimination and harassment are still too often daily experiences for many people.

- The unemployment rate among people from ethnic minorities (19%) is more than twice the rate among white people (8%). 51% of ethnic minority 16-24-year-olds were unemployed in 1994 compared with only 18% of whites.
- On average, pay rates for people from ethnic minorities are 10% less than for white people.
- The proportion of ethnic minority families who are homeless is three times as high as the proportion of white families who are homeless.
- The Home Office has accepted that there may be as many as 130,000 racially motivated incidents in a year.

No one can afford to ignore these problems.

Racial discrimination defined

The Race Relations Act 1976 defines two types of racial discrimination – direct discrimination and indirect discrimination.

Direct discrimination

Direct discrimination refers to a situation where one person treats another person less favourably than another on racial grounds. So, for example, the publican in the Highlands who put up a sign over the bar stating 'No English Served' was unlawfully directly discriminating against English people.

Segregation, separating people of one ethnic group from another, is deemed less favourable treatment, and is therefore classed as direct discrimination, for which there is no acceptable justification.

Therefore, for example, a housing provider who offers accommodation in a particular block, or on a particular scheme, to just black or ethnic minority people, thereby segregating them from the wider white population, even if their reason for doing so was in order to 'protect' ethnic minority people from potential harassment, will be deemed as acting unlawfully, even if there is no detriment to the individuals concerned.

Indirect discrimination

Indirect discrimination occurs where there is a rule, policy, practice or condition that is applied to everyone equally but in practice impacts unequally upon people of one racial or ethnic group. In addition, for the rule, policy, practice or condition to be unlawful indirect discrimination, there has to be no acceptable justification for the practice and the fact that people from a particular racial group cannot comply with the requirement must have a detrimental effect upon them. An example of indirect discrimination in which a justification was accepted is the police height restrictions which were enforced until recently. The police argued successfully that the height requirement was essential as that to be a police officer, one needed physical presence.

For anyone interested in the Race Relations Act 1976, a Guide can be obtained from the Commission for Racial Equality.

Racist attacks and harassment

More than one government and police report has proved that ethnic minorities suffer more from attacks purely motivated by racism than other groups. Some of these are very serious, with people being killed or badly injured. One of the best known cases in recent years has been Stephen Lawrence, a black teenager from Greenwich in London, waiting at a bus stop. He was beaten to death by a group of five young white men who had never seen him before. No one was brought to justice for this murder, and it has made black people in the area feel less safe and reduced their faith in the police to protect them.

Sometimes it's people's houses that are attacked, or their places of worship.

The British Crime Survey in 1997 estimated that about 130,000 racially motivated crimes were committed against black and Asian people, with no particular group 'getting it' worse than another. Half of those who reported harassment to the police felt dissatisfied with what happened next.

More young people get harassed than older ones. People who live in areas where there are few other minorities are more likely to report being harassed than people who live in more mixed areas. The main ethnic minority groups all reported a similar amount of harassment.

A national survey in 1997 worked out that about 250,000 black and Asian people are harassed every year, by workmates, neighbours, but most often by strangers. Usually the people doing the harassing are male. A Health Service report in 1997 showed that black nurses were leaving in large numbers and this was 'linked to harassment in the workplace'.

Racial problems were reported 236 times in Edinburgh schools in 1996.

Most of them were about boys around the age of nine saying or writing racist names, and taking the mickey out of ethnic minority pupils.

In 1998 the Government introduced higher penalties for harassment and assault with a racial motive.

If you are being racially harassed, either physically or with words, the person doing it is probably breaking the law. Don't suffer in silence.

Contact your local Racial Equality Council if there is one (if not, contact the Commission for Racial Equality in London). Contact the police too, with a friend for support. If you're scared and feel you have no one to turn to, phone ChildLine (0800 1111). It's free.

• The above is an extract from the web site http://www.britkid.org
© Britkid

Public attitudes about race

On the whole, white people acknowledge that there is widespread prejudice against ethnic minorities, though fewer white people than in the past say they are prejudiced themselves. A large survey carried out in 1997 found that less than 10% of British people thought people in this country are not at all prejudiced. Asked if they thought people were very prejudiced or quite prejudiced, this is who said 'yes':

Replies				
	White	African-Caribbean	Asian	Jewish
People are very prejudiced	11%	29%	16%	11%
People are quite prejudiced	35%	38%	29%	42%

Most white people mentioned groups who stood out by their colour as likely to experience prejudice, though minorities themselves included Jews. All groups agreed that prejudice against whites was very low.

The reasons people gave for prejudice were, in order of importance:
• the idea that minorities were 'taking jobs'
• various things to do with cultural differences
• believing that minorities were 'getting good housing' and on the dole.

Though they didn't rate it as a big concern, more than half of whites and Asians thought there was too much Asian immigration. Young white people are probably more likely to be hostile towards Asians than towards African-Caribbeans.

On the positive side, over 60% think Asians and African-Caribbeans have made a contribution to public services in Britain. 90% think that Asians have strong family values, 85% think they're hard workers, 77% think they're intelligent and 71% law-abiding. Around 60% rated African-Caribbeans highly on these attributes, as well as thinking they've made a contribution in sport, though only 47% thought they were law-abiding.

• The above is an extract from the web site http://www.britkid.org
© Britkid

Tackling racism

Information from ChildLine

In *Children and Racism*, ChildLine recommended steps to take to help children subjected to racist bullying. These are set out below.

Anti-bullying strategies must address racial harassment

A great deal of the response to problems created elsewhere for children fall to schools. It has to be recognised that this is a great burden, but nowhere else offers the same opportunities for action; and therefore it is a duty. Schools must in their anti-bullying strategies specifically explore the possibility of racial harassment and address the issue through the curriculum and anti-bullying work.

Isolated students need a support structure

This is important in schools, but schools which have only a few children likely to be targeted, because they are racially or nationally different from the majority, clearly need to pay special attention to prevention, using groupwork and the curriculum. Isolated students should be given the name of a designated teacher or senior student to whom they can go with problems and who can carry a pastoral responsibility for the child or children.

Encourage social activities which tackle racism and bullying

All youth organisations, from guiding, scouting and youth clubs to religious and community groups, ought to keep their practice under review to see what can be improved. Organisations like Crime Concern which support schools and communities in trying to promote socially cohesive activities and ways of tackling racism and bullying ought to be promoted and supported.

Involve children: the most under-used resource

Children and young people themselves are the most under-used resource.

Any programme working with the young, if it is to succeed, must involve the children and young people themselves.

Children have the right to a life free of racist abuse

Children need to be offered encouragement to report racial harassment and to view themselves as having the right to a life free of racist abuse. Where children see staff tackling action against bullying, they are more likely to feel able to 'tell'. If children are complaining about racist bullying, it ought to be taken seriously and the impact on children understood. The bullying may have been taking place for a considerable time before the children felt able to tell. It is important to discuss any proposed action with the child, who will be deeply fearful of the consequences of telling. Consideration needs to be given to involving the police where the harassment might breach the law.

Children benefit from discussing and practising coping strategies

It benefits children to discuss and practise coping strategies – in every context. Any child may be put in the position of being a target or a bystander. Since racism is illegal, children and young people need to know they can call the police and that schools have a duty of care to their pupils.

Provide information sources

Schools and youth groups should have available and publicly posted information about sources of help, for example, confidential helplines and local race equality units or racial harassment resources.

Support the most vulnerable

Children experiencing racist abuse in boarding schools and residential institutions are very vulnerable. Preventative work should be undertaken with the student group, and there should be a named teacher or senior student to whom the student can go with problems.

Befriending schemes for youngsters in trouble

Counselling and advice for young people involved in family conflict need to be available within and outside their communities. Some problems are amenable to mediation; others, regrettably, are not.

Befriending schemes for youngsters in trouble with their families might offer a continuing connection with the community so that they do not lose all links with their family background.

Society must unite to oppose racism

It is undeniably important that every aspect of our society unites to oppose racism. The media, press, entertainment industry, sport, community and religious leaders have particularly important roles to play, not only in outlawing racism, but also in providing children and young people with the positive imagery and representation of themselves and their communities which can confirm their confidence in their identity and undermine racist myths.

• The above is an extract from ChildLine's web site which can be found at http://www.childline.org.uk

You have rights against racism

Use them

Have you suffered racial discrimination, harassment or abuse? You don't have to put up with it. You have rights!

Does the law protect me?

Yes. The Race Relations Act makes it illegal to discriminate against anyone on grounds of race, colour, nationality, or national or ethnic origin. It protects people in most situations, such as at work, at school or college, when looking for accommodation or jobs, when going out to pubs and clubs, and so on.

It means that if you think someone has discriminated against you on racial grounds, you may be able to take them to court (or to a tribunal).

What's in it for me?

If you win your case, the discrimination against you will stop. You will also get some financial compensation for the discrimination you have suffered.

The person who has discriminated against you may be made to put things right so it doesn't happen again. The company or organisation where the discrimination took place is responsible for ensuring that everyone is treated the same, regardless of colour, or racial or national origin.

So if you stand up for your rights now, you may stop discrimination and harassment happening in the future, to you or anyone else.

What does the law cover?

The Race Relations Act gives protection against:

Direct discrimination – if you are treated less favourably on racial grounds than other people are treated, or would be treated, in similar circumstances.

A Birmingham night club refused entry to people of ethnic minority origin and their white friends, claiming it was full, yet

admitted all-white groups of people. The club had to pay £20,000 in compensation and introduce an equal opportunities policy after four discrimination cases were taken against it.

A nursing agency in Aberdeen failed to send an application form to a black woman on five separate occasions. A white friend telephoned, and got a form within a few days. The woman complained to an industrial tribunal, and was awarded £2,000 in compensation for direct discrimination.

Indirect discrimination – where a requirement or condition which is applied to everyone actually works as a barrier to people from a particular racial group.

A Liverpool store manager told the careers office that he didn't want job applicants from certain postal districts. These happened to be areas where there were a lot of ethnic minority residents. The industrial tribunal ruled that this was indirect discrimination.

Victimisation – if you are treated unfavourably because you have complained about racial discrimination under the Race Relations Act, or supported someone else who has complained.

A Filipino care assistant applied for a job at a nursing home through the employment service without realising that it was run by a company against which she had already taken a case of racial discrimination. The firm told her she could not be considered for the job because she had accused it of racial discrimination. She complained to an industrial tribunal and won £2,250 in compensation for 'victimisation'.

What should I do?

Act quickly. There are time limits for bringing cases under the Race Relations Act, and racial discrimination can be difficult to prove. You will have a better chance of proving you have been discriminated against if you gather as much evidence as you can, as soon as possible.

Keep a careful, dated record of what happened. The more specific and detailed this is, the better your case will be. Note the names of possible witnesses and, if you can, ask them to make a record of what happened too.

Try to sort it out. Many incidents can be resolved with the support of colleagues or friends by speaking to someone in charge, such as a manager or teacher. Talk about it with someone you trust, and find out if your school or workplace has a racial equality policy.

Seek advice. You can get advice from:
* your local racial equality council (REC)
* a citizens' advice bureau (CAB), or another local advice service or law centre
* your trade union (if the incident was related to work)
* the CRE.

What about harassment and violence?

Racial abuse, harassment and violence are against the law.

You are protected by the Race Relations Act if the abuse occurs at work, at school, when receiving benefits and services, or in any other situation covered by the Race

Relations Act. For example, you can take a case against your employer if you are the target of racism from other employees and the employer does nothing to stop it.

If you are racially harassed by neighbours, their visitors, or others in the local community, you or your local council may be able to get a court order to stop the harassment, and the landlord can take action to get them moved.

If you are racially abused or harassed at a football match, or by another customer in a shop or pub, tell the club, the owner or the store manager to do something about it, and make it clear that it is unacceptable for customers to face racism.

If you are attacked or harassed in the street or in your home, or if you suffer damage to your property, complain to the police.

Racist violence is a serious criminal offence. Any racist attack (including racist intimidation, threats and damage to your property) must be reported to the police immediately.

If you are unsure about what to do – or if you have made a complaint but are not happy with the way it has been dealt with – seek advice. No one should be allowed to get away with racist abuse, harassment or violence.

What else can I do about racism?

Sometimes a few words, to tell someone they are out of order, is all it takes to make them think again. But don't take any chances – and if you think that a situation could get out of hand, get help as quickly as possible.

In some cases, you might be able to get the problem dealt with by complaining direct to the organisation concerned. Many organisations have grievance or complaints procedures, so if you make a complaint direct to the organisation, it should investigate the problem and deal with it.

In other circumstances, where you think you have been badly treated because of your race but there are no procedures to make a formal complaint, a letter to the manager or chief executive of the company may be sufficient. It may prompt them to look into the matter, and make sure it doesn't happen again.

If you don't like what you see or hear in the media, contact the paper or station to complain. If you are not happy with their response, you can also take up the matter with the regulatory body (such as the Press Complaints Commission, Radio Authority, Independent Television Commission, Broadcasting Standards Commission, or BBC Complaints Service).

If you have a problem with the way the police have dealt with you in any situation, note the number of the police officer(s) concerned, complain to their police force, and (in England and Wales) contact the Police Complaints Authority (0171 273 6450).

Who can help?

Don't try and do it all on your own. Talk to someone you can trust, and get support from your family, friends, colleagues or your union. Specialist advisers at RECs, advice services or law centres can also help you to decide whether to make a complaint.

If you have been injured, or if the harassment has made you ill, consult your doctor and, if necessary, get medical evidence.

Remember that the law is there to protect everyone. So stand up for your rights – by doing so, you will help make sure that we can all live in a society where everyone has an equal right to work, learn and live free from discrimination and prejudice, and from the fear of racial harassment and violence.

Where can I get advice?
Racial equality councils (RECs)
There are over 80 RECs covering most areas, working at a local level to tackle discrimination and promote equality of opportunity. Contact details are in local phone books. They are also listed on the CRE's website (http://www.open.gov.uk/cre/crehome.htm).

Advice services and law centres
Contact details can be found in the phone book, at your local library, or from the local council.

Trade unions
Your trade union can help with complaints about racial discrimination or harassment at work.

Commission for Racial Equality (CRE)
A free booklet, *Advice and Assistance from the CRE*, giving further details on the Race Relations Act and on how the CRE can help you, is available from your local CRE office, or from CRE Distribution Services (0171-932 5286).
CRE offices
London: 0171 828 7022
Birmingham: 0121 710 3000
Leeds: 0113 243 4413
Manchester: 0161 831 7782
Edinburgh: 0131 226 5186
Cardiff: 01222 388977
This information has been produced as part of a CRE campaign to encourage more people – both victims and witnesses – to take a stand against racist attitudes and behaviour. For more information about the campaign, contact the CRE on 0171 932 5437.
© Commission for Racial Equality (CRE)

Children and racism

A ChildLine study

The research evidence

We examined calls for the year up to March 31, 1995, to locate records on (i) all children who have identified themselves to ChildLine as black or belonging to an ethnic minority and (ii) all children describing racism, prejudice or 'cultural' issues as a problem for them.

In total 1,616 caller records were selected and reviewed.

Getting help and taking action

'I can't tell Mum and Dad . . . it would upset them.'

'I can't tell my parents . . . they have worked so hard to get me into a good school. They would be terribly upset for me.'

'The other pupils at school are calling me names and making racist remarks. I can't tell my parents because they would go to the school and make a fuss and I'd be called a grass. I was OK at primary school because everyone was treated the same. But there are only five other black people at this school.'

Twenty per cent of the sample had told no one. This was three per cent more than found in the ChildLine bullying study. Thirty-eight per cent had told parents and teachers, 23 per cent had told teachers but not parents and four per cent had told only their parents. The remaining 15 per cent did not say whether or not they had told. Most children described friends knowing and supporting them, but a proportion of children described having no friends. In all then, 42 per cent of this sample said they had told their parents, compared with 71 per cent of callers to the bullying line and 57 per cent of those surveyed in schools as part of the ChildLine study (ChildLine, 1996).

Most children said they did not tell because they feared the bullying would get worse. Just under half of the sample said they could not tell their parents; for them, telling teachers was easier. This was usually to protect their parents. Four main reasons were given by the children: fear that their parents would be hurt and upset; fear that their parents would be worried for them; anxiety that their parents would make a fuss and make things worse; and feeling that their parents had enough to cope with already.

'My dad is black and I get it all the time at school . . . I can't face telling my dad, they call him 'chocolate drop' . . . and other horrible things . . . I don't want to upset him.'

If the racism had driven the youngsters into harbouring feelings of anger, shame and rejection towards their parents, and seeing them as the 'cause' of the problem, this silenced them also.

Sandie, like many of the callers receiving this kind of racism, has begun to feel very bad about herself. During the call she wept, talked about 'wanting to be normal', by which she meant white, and confessed with shame how she feels ashamed of her father.

These responses seemed more prevalent in children who were isolated, without many peers who shared their colour or background, whose family relationships were difficult, and those who were of mixed white and black parentage but had lost the black parent.

Asha, 10, called about 'racial abuse at school'. She said: 'I am the only Asian at the school and there are very few where I live.' She had told a teacher who had confronted the boy but the bullying had continued. Asha's feelings of rejection were exacerbated by her mother's preferential treatment of her brother. 'I feel invisible, like I'm not there.' At the end of the call, she decided to talk to her father about how she felt, and about being able to have contact with other Asian children.

Youngsters mentioned again and again the confidence they felt they would receive from having lots of black children around them. This seemed not only a protection against harassment, but a protective shield against the effects of it, and a support in complaining about it. It is much easier to feel black, Indian or Arab and proud of it, if you are not alone facing gibes, taunts and threats.

Three girls rang together. They were seven and eight years old. They were threatened and bullied by older girls because they were Cypriot. They say: 'Scruffs, go back to your own country.' At the end of the call the girls decided to raise it in class to get support and ideas about how to stop it.

But even if children were isolated, having supportive white friends was comforting and strengthening. Some of the calls made about racist bullying were by white children desperately troubled by the bullying their friends were receiving and asking for advice on how to help. These children's concern demonstrates that children themselves, from all communities, are a resource which schools can use to promote anti-bullying and anti-racist work.

Once they had told parents and teachers, children usually reported getting some support – parents had gone to the school and talked to teachers, and teachers were mainly reported to have been sympathetic and have promised to take action. There were, though, some glaring examples of inaction and dismissal. And even when action was promised, children reported being advised to ignore or not worry about the bullying – something they felt completely unable to do. Who could? Little success in ending the bullying was reported. Teachers commonly promised they would deal with it, giving the child a sense of immediate relief, but nothing identifiable happened and the harassment continued.

Some school responses described seemed highly inappropriate: one child reported having to sit with teachers at lunch, and in the library at other times, to keep him safe. He felt angry that he was seen as the problem rather than those who were doing the bullying.

However effective the support and help was, there was a sense from some children that racism would be a lifelong burden for them. They were not going to let it destroy them; but coping was sometimes a real struggle.

Leanne, 13, called about racism which she described as always going on. 'It's names and saying, "Go home, you shouldn't be here", and sometimes hitting. It has got worse in middle school. I'm scared it will get worse again in senior school.' Leanne had a lot of support at home and felt close to her mother, who would go to the school. Even when things got worse she had felt supported and her mum had never given up. 'School is

beginning to help now, having discussions in assembly and some kids are beginning to listen. But it's not like London with lots of coloured kids.'

She was a tremendously resilient young girl, who usually felt strong and had a close family to help her. But she too said:

'On bad days I feel depressed and kind of dirty and ugly . . . then I'm not so good at coping.'

Leanne's mother was a model of how adults need to respond. Racist bullying can be extremely persistent and in some children's groups it is ingrained. Tackling it is complex and requires more than a one-off reprimand. Children affected need adults 'never to give up' on them.

Some children, though, described receiving a resigned response, basically conveying that this is something they just have to put up with. As one girl said: 'When I told my dad, he just said: "It happens". I don't see why I should have to put up with it though.'

Other young people described being advised to: 'ignore it', 'try to fit in', 'stick up for yourself', 'leave things and see how it goes', 'you need to give proof', and 'stop telling tales'.

According to the children described here, too many adults blithely assume that children ought to be able to stand up to harassment, even when they do not know the full extent of the problem. In ChildLine's experience children often play down the extent of bullying because of shame, self-blame, and anxiety not to upset or displease the adults.

The fact that so many of the calls about racist bullying are from children who are on their own or with very few other similar children suggests that children in more mixed environments may experience less bullying, may find it easier to ask for and get support within their own network, or experience less of an attack on their self-esteem when it can be reinforced by a sense of community. It might also be the case that adults are more alive and responsive to the issue of racist bullying in more mixed environments.

ChildLine's recent study of

bullying behaviour *Why me? Children talking to ChildLine about bullying*, graphically describes the impact bullying has on youngsters, and their difficulty in getting help even when they told, as most of them did. This current study of racist bullying, largely from a different sample of callers (those ringing 0800 1111 rather than our special bullying helplines), conveys exactly the same picture. The lessons to be learned bear repeating.

Racist bullying causes real suffering, affects children's self-esteem and confidence and renders some children and young people so despondent that they feel suicidal or attempt suicide. Youngsters cannot deal with bullying on their own, they need adult help. Verbal assaults can be as damaging as physical attacks. Each school should have a dynamic anti-bullying strategy which confronts all types of bullying. Group techniques involving children and young people themselves are necessary. Though bullying will never be entirely stamped out, this is no excuse for doing nothing – it can be reduced in incidence and severity to the increased well-being of those affected and the entire school community.

Discrimination at school

There were few calls explicitly about discrimination at school. Children who complained to teachers about racist bullying to no effect did feel disregarded and reported that teachers did not take racism seriously. 'They are just the same . . . ', 'They don't like us either . . . ', 'the teacher just laughed when they were on at me . . . ' were some of the comments from children.

Fourteen callers described being blamed for everything, picked on or left out by teachers or dinner ladies because of race.

Benjamin described how he was really trying to sort himself out now, having been in trouble for his behaviour. 'But they don't seem to see I'm trying and I still get blamed for everything. I just feel like giving up.'

Some children calling about school exclusion described this happening because they had responded violently to racist abuse. They felt very aggrieved. Telling children to stand up to bullies can be risky advice.

Children who have a burning sense of having been got at for months can suddenly explode into violence which seems out of proportion. Establishing the rights and wrongs of such an encounter is very difficult for schools.

Street violence

Calls about street violence to children were not common, but shocking. There were 56 in the whole sample.

Lara, 13, rang because that day on the way home from school, she had been set upon by some boys who shouted abuse at her and poured petrol over her head and shoulders. Luckily she was not alone and her friends helped her home. Her mother called the police, who acted swiftly and sensitively. Lara was deeply shaken and very fearful of the walk home from school.

Lara was brave and had acted with real presence of mind. She did not see her attackers as powerful and strong but rather as pathetic; but this did not reduce the physical threat. She was now frightened that she would always feel fear.

Hari, 15, his cousins and friends were being racially abused by a family living opposite them. 'I've lived here all my life and I object to being called a "black bastard".' There are few Asian families in his neighbourhood and he sometimes became so angry he felt he would just have to leave the area or he'd end up doing something criminal. But he was determined not to be harassed out and began to think of contacting the police.

The sense of violent threat can be a constant source of fear to youngsters either because they are verbally abused in the street – by adults as well as other children – or because they are aware of a racist presence. They can find it hard to convince friends or family about how profoundly affected they are.

Jay, 14, rang because she moved to a new area where there are many BNP and National Front supporters and she felt terrorised by their presence. 'The school is not racist and my friends say, "well we're not racist"; but they just don't understand how frightening it is.' Jay did not want to tell her parents because '. . . they have enough to worry about and they'll just start worrying about me.'

Some young people are not so lucky with the police, where the impression is that police are powerless or see themselves as powerless in some areas. Those affected can see them as unwilling to help.

Rashdi, 15, called to ask for help about a neighbour who has been following her. She said it was racially motivated. The persecution was affecting her school work. She was not eating or sleeping. She had told the police who had told her it was a civil matter. He had followed her again the previous day and threatened her. She was now feeling she could not go out at all.

Sarat, 12, rang because he and his family were constantly harassed by a group of boys on their estate. They knew who the boys were and had informed the police, who said they could do nothing because the boys were too young. 'Our car and house windows have been smashed and they throw things. My cousins are also terrified and my mother is scared to come out.' Sarat said he felt safe at school but he was fed up and wanted the violence to stop. He had not known about the local race equality unit and decided to phone them.

In this family, according to the child, police inaction was driving the older brother into thinking he had to do something, the kind of vigilante action whose possible consequences terrified Sarat. Here the seeds of communal violence can be seen growing.

Dealing with these racial conflicts presents youngsters with enormous dilemmas about whose side they are on, and a test of courage which many adults might fail.

One 12-year-old girl called about her alarm over a fight due to take place between gangs of white and black youngsters at her school. She was too frightened to tell the teacher in case she was found out and attacked as a grass. In the end she decided she had to tell so the fight could be stopped.

Children and young people called about racial harassment involving phone calls and letters, graffiti, verbal abuse in the streets and at the house, stone throwing, wrecked possessions, broken windows and fireworks through the letterbox. As one child said:

'The mums here are as bad as the kids.'
© *ChildLine*
January, 1998

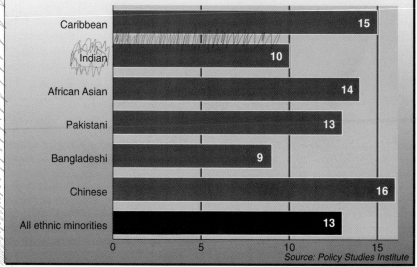

Britain's ethnic mix

The Policy Studies Institute survey of ethnic minorities suggests that 250,000 people a year are victims of racial harassment, including insults and abuse by strangers, workmates, neighbours and the police, as well as more serious attacks.

Per cent subjected to racial harassment over the last 12 months

Caribbean	15
Indian	10
African Asian	14
Pakistani	13
Bangladeshi	9
Chinese	16
All ethnic minorities	13

Source: Policy Studies Institute

An anti-racist charter for the new millennium

Summary

The fascist right can only be permanently defeated on the basis of an agenda which centrally tackles racism at its roots

Racism today has become the most serious threat to the democratic fabric of society since the 1930s. Defeating racism, and the right-wing extremists who feed on it, is a precondition for the preservation of human and democratic rights into the next millennium.

Racism today is directed against Asian, Caribbean, African and other Black communities, immigrants, asylum seekers, Jewish people and other minorities. Racism takes the form of racist murders, attacks and abuse, arson against property, attacks on places of worship, attacks on the rights of immigrants and asylum seekers, discrimination in employment and service provision and institutional racism.

Every concession to racism by mainstream political parties and institutions legitimises it and encourages its most dangerous exponents on the streets and in the parties of the extreme racist right. The fascist right can only be permanently defeated on the basis of an agenda which centrally tackles racism at its roots.

To create a movement capable of confronting and destroying racism requires unity – unity between Asians, Caribbeans and Africans and unity between Black communities, the Jewish community and other oppressed groups and communities,

the trade unions and labour movement, churches and faiths and all organisations and individuals prepared to take a stand against racism. Such a movement requires, and must respect, the central importance of Black self-organisation and leadership of the anti-racist struggle, as the embodiment of the core contribution of the communities, families and individuals who actually confront racism. No anti-racist movement can be successful without recognising the contribution to be made by all sections of society and especially seeking to ensure the fullest participation of women, young people, lesbians and gay men, disabled people and all those facing oppression and discrimination.

To these ends we call for:

1. Unity in the struggle against racism and the fascists. Action, including legal measures and community action, against racial violence and harassment.

2. Immigration and asylum rights free of racism.

3. Positive action against racial discrimination in employment and education. Equal political representation of minority communities at least proportional to their numbers in society.

4. No place for fascists in a democratic society.

5. Freedom of religion and religious tolerance. The right to self-organisation for Black and minority communities in all fields of life, and the leading role of those oppressed by racism, the Black and other minority communities, in the anti-racist struggle

6. Solidarity with all peoples struggling against racism and imperialism across the globe.

7. The celebration of a multicultural society.

• The above is an extract from the BLINK (Black Information Link) web site which can be found at http://www.blink.org.uk, produced by The 1990 Trust.

© The 1990 Trust

Don't shut your eyes

Take a stand against racism

It would be easy to think that racism barely exists in Britain today. Our cities, schools, offices and shops are filled with people of all colours, cultures and national and ethnic backgrounds. People from ethnic minorities are successful in business, politics, the arts, sports and almost any other area you care to think about. Employers have equal opportunity policies promising to treat everyone fairly, and racial discrimination, harassment and abuse are against the law.

Yet racism still exists.

- Incidents of racial harassment and abuse occur every day – and sometimes these escalate into sickening racist violence, such as the killing of Stephen Lawrence.
- Despite the law, people are still being discriminated against because of the colour of their skin, their race or their ethnic background.
- And people still make judgements about others based on prejudice and racial or national stereotypes.

The consequences of such prejudice and discrimination are that people from ethnic minority groups are still treated as second-class citizens in many walks of life.

- 13% of people from ethnic minority groups were unemployed in Spring 1998, compared with 5.7% of white people.
- Black people in some areas are eight times more likely to be stopped and searched by the police than white people, according to a 1998 report.
- The number of racial incidents recorded by the police rose to 13,917 in 1996/97. Many more go unreported.
- The 1996 British Crime Survey estimated that 143,000 crimes committed against black and Asian people were motivated by racism.
- Over 10,000 people contacted the CRE in 1997 for advice about racial discrimination – and 1,661 people actually applied for legal assistance with their case.
- Black Caribbean pupils are five times more likely to be excluded from school than white pupils, according to figures for English schools in 1995/96.

What can you do?

It doesn't have to be this way. If you think racism is wrong, you can do something about it.

The vast majority of people do not make racist remarks, and would never racially abuse anyone. But most of us can probably remember times when we witnessed racist behaviour and did nothing to stop it. Maybe it was an incident at work, or a comment overheard in the pub, or jokes and insults directed at other passengers on a bus or a train. It might even have come from a friend or relative, or a colleague, someone we respected. So we let it go. We didn't want to make a fuss. What difference would it make anyway?

The answer is: it can make all the difference.

By not speaking up you let others believe that their behaviour is acceptable. By speaking out, you can make them think about their words and actions. You may even stop them doing it again.

Sometimes all it takes is a few quiet words to persuade someone they are out of order.

On other occasions – such as at work, or at a meeting, or in a

> **By not speaking up you let others believe that their behaviour is acceptable. By speaking out, you can make them think about their words and actions**

classroom – you may need to make a formal complaint to an organisation, or testify on behalf of someone who has been victimised. It always helps to make a note of what has happened, including the date and time, so that you can remember them later on.

If you see someone being harassed, or overhear someone making racist remarks – maybe in the canteen at work, or in the playground at school, or at a sports or leisure centre – tell someone, such as a manager or teacher. They are responsible for doing something about it.

If someone is being racially abused or attacked in the street or another public place, you should report the incident directly to the police, without delay.

Be careful that you do not do anything that will put yourself or anyone else in danger. If you think a situation could get out of hand, get help as quickly as possible.

If you hear racist chanting at a football match, or another sports event, report it to the club or the appropriate sports authority.

If you see racist graffiti on a building, train or bus, complain to the owners and ask for it to be removed.

If you think a TV or radio programme, an advertisement or a newspaper article is insulting to people from a certain ethnic group, don't just shrug your shoulders – complain. Write to the editor, producer or company involved, and if you don't know their name, or aren't satisfied with their response, take it up with the relevant agency (listed below).

It's up to all of us, whatever our colour or race, to make sure racist behaviour and attitudes are not accepted in Britain. It's our responsibility, whether we are directors of companies, editors of newspapers, members of parliament, or ordinary members of the public.

The human and social costs of

racial discrimination, prejudice and hatred are too high for us to do nothing. We can all do something to make a difference.

Things won't change on their own. Everyone needs to do the right thing, and take a stand against racism.

Racial discrimination

The Race Relations Act makes it unlawful to discriminate against anyone because of their race, colour, nationality, or national or ethnic origin. This law protects people in most situations, such as at work, at school, when looking for housing, applying for benefits, going shopping or out to pubs and clubs, and so on. But it can only work if the person who makes a complaint can count on colleagues or witnesses to come forward and give evidence.

When a barmaid objected to being told by her boss not to serve black customers, she suddenly found herself out of a job. The CRE helped her to claim compensation and took action against the pub landlord for giving 'discriminatory instructions'.

When 17 year-old Kelly Turner heard an ex-boyfriend bragging about beating up and seriously injuring an Asian teenager in a racist attack, she told the police. Her evidence helped to get the offenders arrested and sentenced.

When a passenger on a London bus heard the driver racially abusing a black woman who was looking for change to pay her fare, he complained to the bus company. The driver was disciplined.

When telesales workers at a Leeds kitchen design company were told not to sell to Asian families, a white part-time employee reported this to his Asian colleague, a fellow student, who had been absent when the instruction was given. Both resigned in protest, told their local paper, and took the company to an industrial tribunal.

An elderly couple complained to Wembley Stadium about racist abuse directed at Chilean players during an international football match. The management investigated the offenders with the intention of banning them from future matches, and gave the couple free tickets and a tour of the ground.

Who do you contact?

- For general advice on racial discrimination or harassment contact your local racial equality council (REC), citizens' advice bureau or other advice centre (the numbers are in your local telephone book).
- Complaints about discrimination should be reported to your REC, your trade union (and/or a senior manager), a law centre, an advice centre, or the CRE.
- Incidents of racial harassment or abuse in the street or other public places should be reported immediately to the police.
- If you have a problem with the way the police have dealt with any member of the public, note the number of the police officer(s) concerned, complain to their police force, and (in England and Wales) contact the Police Complaints Authority (0171 273 6450).
- If you hear racist abuse or chanting at a sports event, contact a steward, the police, the club concerned, or the sport's governing body. If it happens at a football match, you can also contact the campaign Kick It Out (0171 288 6012).

- Complaints about racially offensive material in the media should be reported to one of the following bodies:
Press Complaints Commission: 0171 353 1248
Advertising Standards Authority: 0171 580 5555
Radio Authority: 0171 430 2724
Independent Television Commission: 0171 255 3000
Broadcasting Standards Commission: 0171 233 0544
BBC Complaints Service:
Radio: 0171 580 4468
Television: 0181 743 8000
CRC Offices:
London: 0171 828 7022
Birmingham: 0121 710 3000
Leeds: 0113 243 4413
Manchester: 0161 831 7782
Edinburgh: 0131 226 5186
Cardiff: 01222 388977
- This information has been produced as part of a CRE campaign to encourage more people – both victims and witnesses – to take a stand against racist attitudes and behaviour. For more information about the campaign, contact the CRE on 0171-932 5437. Or see page 41 for address details.

© Commission for Racial Equality (CRE)

Regions of residence

Greater London contains nearly half (45%) of Britiain's non-white population compared with only 10% of the white popuation

	White		Ethnic minorities	
	No.	% of GB	No.	% of GB
South east	15,513,800	29.9	1,694,700	56.4
Greater London	*5,332,900*	*10.3*	*1,346,800*	*44.8*
East Anglia	1,983,700	3.8	43,300	1.4
South west	4,546,900	8.8	62,700	2.1
West Midlands	2,179,200	9.1	422,900	14.1
West Midlands MC	*2,179,200*	*4.2*	*372,500*	*12.4*
East Midlands	3,764,500	7.3	188,800	6.3
Yorks & Humberside	4,621,200	8.9	215,200	7.2
North west	6,000,400	11.6	243,200	8.1
Greater Manchester	*2,351,900*	*4.5*	*147,500*	*4.9*
Merseyside	*1,378,300*	*2.7*	*25,300*	*0.8*
North	2,989,000	5.8	37,800	1.3
Tyne & Wear	*1,075,500*	*2.1*	*19,700*	*0.7*
Wales	2,773,900	5.4	41,200	1.4
Scotland	4,934,500	9.5	64,000	2.1
Total	**51,843,900**	**100.0**	**3,006,500**	**100.0**

Source: Owen, D (1992-1995) 1991 Census Statistical Papers 1-9, Centre for Research in Ethnic Relations, University of Warwick/CRE

EU set to accept anti-racism law

By Stephen Bates in Brussels

Plans for Europe-wide anti-racism legislation, partly based on the example of British law, are likely to be accepted by the European Commission in Brussels today.

The proposals, put forward by Padraig Flynn, the Irish social affairs commissioner, would provide a framework to outlaw racism and discrimination in jobs, housing, education, sport and media. They are being welcomed by the Government, in stark contrast to its Conservative predecessor which opposed what it saw as EU interference in an area where Britain already had regulations.

The EC move is a first attempt to put into force part of last year's Amsterdam Treaty, which contains a clause intended to combat discrimination 'based on sex, racial or ethnic origin, religion or belief, disability, age or sexual orientation'.

It is likely to be hotly contested in Europe. Openly racist parties have made big gains in France and Denmark. An EU-wide survey last year found a third of the 16,000 people questioned openly admitting feeling quite or very racist.

The commission plan may also open the first breach over an issue of European regulations between Labour and the Tories. After signing up to the EU social chapter's initial regulations on working hours and parental leave, the Government has so far been cautious about accepting any more European intervention in the social field.

> **'While the prime responsibility for combating racism lies with member states, the transnational dimension of the problem justifies action at European level'**

The document, which could be adopted across Europe by the end of next year, calls for each of the 15 member states to adopt legislation outlawing racism and discrimination in employment and social policy and areas such as sport and the media. It says: 'While the prime responsibility for combating racism lies with member states, the transnational dimension of the problem justifies action at European level.'

Practice in Europe varies widely, with some, such as the Netherlands, having anti-racist clauses written into their constitutions and others having scarcely any regulations. In France, in areas controlled by the National Front, local officials are removing legislation allowing equal access to minority groups, while even in socially-liberal Denmark, openly racist politicians won 10 per cent of the vote in the recent general election with demands for the repatriation of black immigrants.

The commission wants to see measures to promote integration of groups such as gypsies, refugees and migrant workers. It suggests EU structural funds might be targeted to improving the integration of excluded groups.

It calls for the media to ensure information is free from stereotyping and prejudice.

© The Guardian
March, 1998

Percentage in each ethnic group who had suffered different types of crime

A higher proportion of black people were victims of both household and personal offences in 1993 than people from other ethnic groups. Twenty-six per cent of black car owners had suffered theft either of or from their vehicle in 1993, compared with 20 per cent of white car owners. 13 per cent of black households had been burgled, twice the proportion of white households.

	Black	Indian	Bangladeshi/ Pakistani	White
	%	%	%	%
Household offences	36	35	34	33
Vehicle vandalism*	12	9	11	8
Vehicle theft*	26	22	25	20
Burglary	13	10	6	6
Vandalism	4	4	5	4
Other household offences	9	7	11	10
Personal offences	13	9	10	8
Assaults	7	2	4	4
Threats	4	2	4	3
Robbery from person	3	3	4	2
Other theft	5	4	2	4

* Percentage of vehicle owners

Source: British Crime Survey 1994, from ONS 1996

14

Stopped 60 times, never arrested

The police are eight times more likely to stop a black man than a white. Just ask Oluwa. By Sebastian Naidoo

His first time was at the age of 15. By his late teens he'd lost track of how many prickly encounters he'd had. Ten years later he reckons it happens about once a month. And now he hardly breaks out in a sweat.

'There's never been a reason for me to run into the police,' says 27-year-old Oluwa Kubweza from behind the wheel of his black Vitara jeep. 'I've never been arrested or taken into custody. My cars have always been legal. I've got to the stage where I say as little as possible. I know the score. I give them my details, and ask for the producer,' he says.

Mr Kubweza has been stopped more than 60 times over the past six years. He is a physics graduate and is currently working as a sales executive for a Surrey advertising company. He is also a regular at his local police station in Tottenham, north London, where he goes to 'produce' his driving licence and insurance documents when asked.

'I try to rationalise their behaviour. I've asked several times whether they're stopping me because I'm black. They say they're just doing routine checks,' he says. 'Once when I asked, we ended up in verbal abuse. He swore at me, saying all blacks are muggers.'

On another occasion, a gun was wielded over him by a plain-clothes officer who had pursued him along a London artery in a high-speed chase on his way home from a night-shift at work.

At times, Mr Kubweza threads through side streets to avoid patrolled areas. When security was tightened after bomb blasts in the City and Docklands areas of London, he was persistently stopped and searched at a string of checkpoints.

Black people are up to eight

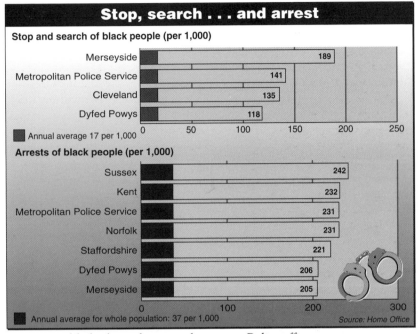

Stop, search . . . and arrest

Stop and search of black people (per 1,000)

Region	per 1,000
Merseyside	189
Metropolitan Police Service	141
Cleveland	135
Dyfed Powys	118

Annual average 17 per 1,000

Arrests of black people (per 1,000)

Region	per 1,000
Sussex	242
Kent	232
Metropolitan Police Service	231
Norfolk	231
Staffordshire	221
Dyfed Powys	206
Merseyside	205

Annual average for whole population: 37 per 1,000

Source: Home Office

times more likely than white people to be stopped and searched, according to a recent analysis of Home Office data by Statewatch, an independent police monitor. The first detailed ethnic breakdown of police stops and searches across England and Wales showed over 100 stops and searches of black people per 1,000 of the local black population in Cleveland, Dyfed Powys, Merseyside and the Met. There were less than 50 stops and searches of white people per 1,000 in the same areas.

A Home Office report published a few weeks ago shows that a disproportionate number of arrests of black people are dropped due to weak evidence. It explains: 'The police sometimes view members of ethnic minority groups and black people in particular as "problematic".'

Maurice McLeod, a 29-year-old black journalist, kept a meticulous record of his stop and search encounters. They totalled 31 during the first three months of 1995, usually on the same west London route. He was never arrested.

Police officers can carry out stop and search only if they have reasonable grounds for suspicion. They are obliged by law to fill out an incident form and tell a suspect of their right to a copy of the record.

'There is no legal reason for the stop and search of young black men in a majority of these cases,' says human rights lawyer Sadiq Khan, who has dealt with about 50 cases of police misconduct stemming from stops and searches. 'I have no doubt that this constitutes harassment.' Mr Khan estimates that up to 80 per cent of his clients are young black men, vulnerable to wrongful arrests.

'We've plainly said we are stopping too many young black men for insufficiently good reasons,' says former Lambeth Chief Inspector and borough liaison officer Alan O'Gorman. 'If we can demonstrate . . . That we're working on it, public confidence will be greater, and [so will] the degree to which we police by consent.'

Two routes are open to aggrieved people seeking a challenge

against a police officer for what they believe to be abuse of power. Formal complaints – investigated by officers from a separate force under the supervision of the Police Complaints Authority (PCA) – offer the prospect of an officer being disciplined or criminally prosecuted. Of the 258 complaints for breaches of stop and search rules recorded by the PCA for the year until the end of last March: no officer was disciplined, 14 were 'admonished'.

It takes civil action for compensation against a police employer – usually a Chief Constable – to put stop and search records before a jury. Legal aid is available for the process, which can take as long as six years to complete. Court guidelines now limit damages to £50,000, awarded according to the severity of an abuse. An officer usually returns to work after a case is settled.

'What's the point of making a complaint? If I was lucky I'd get an insincere apology,' says Mr Kubweza.

'Police officers freely interpret their code of conduct. I don't want a stop and search to depend on whether a particularly progressive officer is on duty,' says Lee Jasper, who heads a black community group, the 1990

Trust. Making policy and practice match in this area is the job of a Home Office quango called the Specialist Support Unit, which has trained about 2,000 senior police officers in 'equality objectives'.

'Our training starts from the premise that all police officers might have stereotyped perceptions that influence their behaviour [during a] stop and search,' says the support unit's director and chief trainer Jerome Mack.

Trainees memorise 10 commandments guaranteed to prevent conflict during a stop and search. In particular; they learn to avoid telling suspects to shut up or stand absolutely still, calling the suspect names, showing disrespect and assuming that lack of eye contact indicates guilt.

Using role play and video to show reasonable grounds for a stop and search, the two-day cross-cultural course trains high-ranking officers how to identify suspicious behaviour in black communities. These officers are expected to pass on the skills.

But from next week, PCs on the beat in the south London borough of Lambeth will get a direct lesson from Mr Mack. They will soon be reciting

the 10 commandments as part of a fresh bid by the local police community consultative group to crush 'bad apples' in the station and stamp out bad attitude on the street.

Set in motion by Lord Scarman's recommendations following clashes in Brixton and Tottenham during the first half of the Eighties, and fuelled by concerns over zero tolerance tactics and the kind of policing for which the Notting Hill Carnival gained notoriety, the Lambeth consultative group has thrashed out its own peace plan.

The Community and Race Relations strategy puts local people on a committee to help steer key decisions about police recruitment, training and tackling institutionalised racism. It may become a model for other forces.

But not everyone is convinced. Mr Kubweza for one will need a bit more persuasion: 'I grew up with the hassle. The longer it goes on, the more I just see the uniform. My only encounters have been negative. It's made me very anti-police. That's what experience has taught me. I can't see any way it's going to change.'

First published in The Independent September, 1998

Let us tackle racism together urges Jack Straw

Tackling racism, prejudice, and discrimination is not just a national responsibility but an individual one as well, Home Secretary Jack Straw told an EU conference in Manchester today.

Addressing the EU Presidency conference, 'Europe against Racism', Mr Straw told delegates that racism did not respect national borders:

'All European countries suffer from racism and I am in no doubt that there is a crucial role for European action to tackle it.

'I have long been involved in the fight against racism, xenophobia and anti-Semitism. I am greatly encouraged by the extent to which concern about it has risen up the European agenda in recent years.'

Mr Straw added: 'Tackling racism, prejudice and discrimination is an individual responsibility which we all bear in both our personal and professional lives. It is also a national responsibility – governments have an essential role to play in combating racism, xenophobia and anti-Semitism within their own borders.

'Everyone agrees on what we want to achieve – a stable and secure Europe with equal rights and equal opportunities.

'Societies differ from country to country throughout the European Union. But we all share common values and a common vision of inclusive societies of mutual respect and tolerance.

'But warm words are not enough.

Our vision needs to be translated into concrete action to give everyone, whatever their colour or background, a real chance to better themselves and their families.'

Government officials and representatives of non-governmental organisations from each of the 15 member states attended the two-day conference. Delegates discussed the possibilities and opportunities for Europe-wide action to combat racism, xenophobia and anti-Semitism to maintain the momentum established by the European Year Against Racism.

The 'Europe against Racism' seminar is one of a number of seminars organised as part of the UK Presidency of the European Union.

© Crown Copyright, 1998

Racial discrimination in employment

This article provides some basic details of employment law. It does not attempt to describe every detail, and should not be taken as an authoritative statement of the law. More detailed information is provided in the booklets listed below.

The Race Relations Act 1976 makes racial discrimination unlawful in employment, vocational training and related areas. The Act applies in Great Britain but not in Northern Ireland.

The Act defines racial discrimination as discrimination on the grounds of colour, race, nationality, or ethnic or national origins.

There are two types of racial discrimination – generally referred to as direct and indirect.

Direct discrimination arises where one person treats another less favourably, on racial grounds, than he or she treats (or would treat) someone else. In deciding whether a particular kind of treatment may constitute direct racial discrimination it is necessary to consider:

- whether the treatment was any less favourable compared to the treatment which was (or would be) accorded to another person, and if so;
- whether the unfavourable treatment was due to the colour, race, nationality or ethnic or national origins of the person who was less favourably treated, or of someone else connected with that person (for example, their spouse).

It is not necessary to show that unfavourable treatment on racial grounds was openly intended: often it will be possible to infer that discrimination was intended, from the circumstances in which the treatment occurred.

Indirect discrimination is treatment that may be equal in the sense that it applies to employees of different racial groups, but which is discriminatory in its effect on one particular racial group. It occurs when one person applies, to another person, a condition or requirement with which he or she must comply to gain a benefit or to avoid a disadvantage.

However, such a condition will not be indirectly discriminatory unless all the following are true:

- it applies, or would apply, equally to other employees whatever their racial group;
- the proportion of people in the disadvantaged person's racial group who can comply with it is considerably smaller than the proportion of those not in that group who can comply;
- it is detrimental to the complainant because he or she cannot comply with it;
- the employer cannot show it to be a justifiable condition or requirement irrespective of the colour, race, nationality or ethnic or national origins of the person to whom it is applied.

Segregation of a person from others on racial grounds is a further form of discrimination.

It is also unlawful to treat someone less favourably than others because they have asserted their rights under race equality law or have assisted someone else to do so. Such discrimination is called victimisation.

In addition, it is contrary to the Act to publish an advertisement indicating an intention to discriminate on grounds of colour, race, nationality or ethnic or national origins.

The Criminal Justice and Public Order Act 1994 created a new offence of intentionally causing harassment, alarm or distress through the use of threatening, abusive or insulting behaviour, words or displays. The new offence could apply where the harassment is racially motivated. Convictions may result in imprisonment, a heavy fine or both.

How the Race Relations Act works

It is unlawful for an employer to discriminate:

- in recruitment: including arrangements for deciding who should be offered employment;
- in the terms offered or by refusing or deliberately omitting to offer a person employment;
- in terms and conditions: during employment;
- in access to, or by denial of, opportunities: for promotion, transfer, training or any other benefits, schemes, facilities or services;
- by dismissing an employee or causing him or her any other detriment.

An employer may also be liable for an act of unlawful discrimination by an agent or any of his employees. The employer may not be liable if he or she can prove that he took reasonable steps to prevent his or her employees acting in such a way.

Exceptions from the Act

There are instances where being a member of a particular racial group is a Genuine Occupational Qualification. For example:

- where a person of a particular racial group is required for a job involving participation in a dramatic performance or as a photographic model;
- where the jobholder provides to people of a particular racial group personal services providing their welfare and those services can most effectively be provided by a person of the same racial group.

Other exceptions, known as positive action, can help members of underrepresented racial groups compete on equal terms with others in the labour market. An employer or training body may, for example, encourage members of a particular racial group to apply for particular work; or may provide special training to equip such people better in particular work, where in either case people of that group are under-represented in that work.

Acts done under statutory authority or to safeguard national security are also permitted under the terms of the Act.

Responsibility for the Act

The Department for Education and Employment (DfEE) is responsible for aspects of the Act relating to employment. The Department promotes racial equality through its publications and through its Race Relations Employment Advisory Service. The Advisory Service can be contacted at its Head Office at 14th Floor, Cumberland House, 200 Broad Street, Birmingham B15 1TA. Tel: 0121 244 8141/2/3.

The Commission for Racial Equality (CRE) was set up under the 1976 Act. CRE staff can advise on good practice in racial equality. The Commission has also issued a Code of Practice in employment which

industrial tribunals must take into account in deciding cases (see 'Complaints' below). In addition, the Commission has the discretion to assist those who consider they may have been discriminated against.

The CRE can be contacted at its Head Office at Elliot House, 10-12 Allington Street, London SW1E 5EH.

Complaints

Anyone who considers that he or she has been discriminated against in employment on grounds of race may make a complaint to an industrial tribunal.

Complaints should be made within 3 months of the date when the alleged discrimination took place. The Advisory, Conciliation and Arbitration Service (ACAS) has a statutory duty to conciliate in these complaints. If there is no resolution through conciliation, direct discussions between the parties, or withdrawal by the applicant, then the complaint will proceed to a tribunal hearing. If the tribunal agrees that discrimination has taken place it may then:

- declare the rights of the parties involved;
- require the respondent to pay compensation to the complainant;
- recommend that the respondent take particular action to remove or reduce the effect on the complainant of the discrimination that took place.

• This article is an extract of one of a series on employment rights produced for small employers, produced for the DfEE.

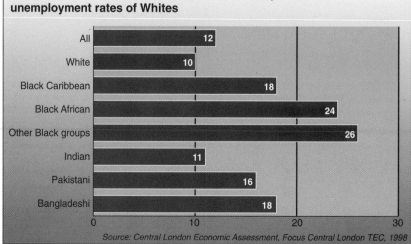

Unemployment rates by ethnic groups in the Inner London area

In 1997 around a quarter of all economically active Black Africans and other Black groups were unemployed, compared to just 10% of Whites. Bangladeshis and Black Caribbeans have nearly twice the unemployment rates of Whites

Group	Rate
All	12
White	10
Black Caribbean	18
Black African	24
Other Black groups	26
Indian	11
Pakistani	16
Bangladeshi	18

Source: Central London Economic Assessment, Focus Central London TEC, 1998

Equality for all

Winning race equality at work

Getting started

This information is a practical guide to negotiating race equality at work. It includes handy references to the law, as well as examples of agreements won by Transport & General Workers' Union (T&G) representatives in a range of workplaces up and down the country.

Winning race equality in the workplace is one of the most important challenges facing trade unions today. This information will help you get started.

As a matter of fact . . .

The T&G estimates that about one in ten members are black or belong to an ethnic minority. Black women are more likely to belong to a union than white women while the reverse is true for men. Source: Labour Force Survey 1989.

Recruitment, promotion and selection

The 'colour bar' is still alive and kicking in British industry. Word of mouth and other informal methods of recruitment and promotion mean that black people may never get the chance to compete for a job. But a failure to advertise openly could be against the law. The Commission for Racial Equality (CRE) Code of Practice says: 'employers should not confine advertisements to those areas or publications which would exclude or disproportionately reduce the numbers of applicants from a particular racial group.' (CRE Code 1.6a)

- Where an employer has an internal advertising procedure, try winning agreement to simultaneous internal and external advertising.
- Urge the employer to advertise jobs in the black press as a way of increasing applications from black people. But remind them not to expect instant results. It takes a while for a workplace with a 'whites-only' reputation to build up credibility as an equal opportunity employer.
- Ads should carry an equal opportunity commitment and can encourage underrepresented groups to apply. They should also make it crystal clear that comparable qualifications and skills gained abroad are acceptable.
- Tell the employer to avoid making unnecessary requirements, such as length of residence or experience, which may deter black people from applying.
- If your employer recruits through a particular employment agency, job centre or school, check whether it means that black people are less likely to apply.
- Clear job descriptions and person specifications are vital. Staff involved in shortlisting and interviewing should be informed of selection criteria and given appropriate training on the effects of prejudice on selection decisions.

As a matter of fact . . .

About one-third of private employers discriminate against black applicants by refusing them an interview while offering one to equally qualified whites.

Source: Employment Institute, Economic Report, June 1990.

Passing the test

IQ, 'psychometric' and personality tests are employers' latest recruitment fad. The quasi-scientific appearance of such tests may conceal in-built race bias. In a recent case backed by the CRE, a British Rail test based on principles common throughout industry was shown to discriminate against people who speak English as a second language.

- Check that selection tests and criteria are strictly related to job requirements and are not designed in such a way as to make it harder for ethnic minority groups to pass. (CRE Code 1.13)

As a matter of fact . . .

Black people are one and a half times more likely to be unemployed than whites. The unemployment rate for black youth is double that for whites.
Source: *Employment Gazette* Feb/April 1991

Genuine occupational qualification

Selection on racial grounds is allowed in certain jobs where being of a particular racial group is a genuine occupational qualification for that job. The CRE Code of Practice gives the example of where a job involves providing a racial group with personal services promoting their welfare. (CRE Code 1.15)

The colour of money

The simple fact is that black workers are lower paid than whites. According to the PSI survey, 'Black and White in Britain', on average black men earn 85% of white men's gross weekly pay. Although the gap between black and white women's weekly earnings is much smaller, this is partly because black women work longer hours.*

Black people are concentrated in the lowest-paying industries and jobs. Unequal training and promotion opportunities confirm black workers' poor status. So, many of the tried and tested union demands around ending low pay will directly benefit black workers.

But there is another problem negotiators need to address and that is the low value attached to black people's work. As with sex, a worker's race can colour society's view of how much a job is worth. Black women's work is often treated as the lowest skilled of all.

Ethnic monitoring of the pay and grading structure is vital. Over-representation of black workers in the lowest grades suggests that discrimination has occurred and is a powerful argument for positive action.

For example, at Ford black workers are concentrated in the lowest paying grades.

There is leverage in both the equal pay and race discrimination laws to tackle bias in pay (CRE Code 1.20) but the biggest gains can be won through negotiation using the checklist below:

- Find out where black workers are in the pay and grading structure.
- Aim to abolish or consolidate the lowest grades.
- Aim to improve basic pay.
- Look at how much black women earn and if you think there may be pay discrimination on the grounds of sex, use the equal value laws to back up your argument to management.

Racial harassment

Racial harassment, from so-called 'jokes' to physical assault, creates a climate of fear and intimidation. It damages black workers' health, threatens their job security and undermines equality at work. The harasser can be the employer, a supervisor, colleague or member of the public.

Black women may face a combination of racial and sexual harassment and procedures will need to take account of this. The TGWU Legal Department and the Equal Opportunities Commission can advise on using the Sex Discrimination Act.

Harassment can amount to unlawful race discrimination under the Race Relations Act. It may be appropriate to suggest that you write a letter to the harasser asking them to stop. Remember to keep a copy of the letter and details of any response.

As a matter of fact . . .

The CRE estimates that there is a race attack of some kind every 7.5 minutes in England and Wales.

The TUC defines racial harassment as:

- Abusive language and racist 'jokes'
- Racial name-calling
- Display of racially offensive written or visual material including graffiti
- Physical threats, assault and

insulting or abusive behaviour or gestures
- Open hostility to black workers, including organised hostility in the workplace
- Unfair allocation of work and responsibilities
- Exclusion from normal workplace conversation or social events, i.e. being 'frozen out'.

Prevention is better than cure

It's in everyone's interest to put a stop to racist language and behaviour before it ever gets to the stage of formal procedures. To challenge racism takes courage and individual members must feel confident that, when they do, the union is right there beside them.

Harassment is less likely to flourish where the union encourages open discussion about equal opportunities and is involved in practical and anti-racist activity, in and out of the workplace.

- Remember, your TGWU regional race advisory committee will be happy to talk to you informally or provide speakers

Grievance and disciplinary procedures

A statement and procedure for dealing with racial harassment can be built into a joint union-management equal opportunities agreement.

The statement should be widely publicised to the workforce and:
- Define racial harassment (see above)
- Stress that racial harassment will not be tolerated and, in cases such as assault, can amount to gross misconduct, leading to redeployment or dismissal
- State that racial harassment is a

disciplinary offence which will be dealt with under agreed grievance and disciplinary procedures
- Set out procedures for dealing with complaints of racial harassment
- Explain that grievances will be handled with speed and confidentiality and that, where appropriate, the harasser, and not the victim, will be relocated
- Encourage victims of harassment to approach their union representative and list other sources of help, for example the CRE
- Identify the senior member of management who has been allocated responsibility for race equality issues
- Make a commitment to provide suitable training for staff involved in operating procedures.

Existing grievance and disciplinary procedures will need to be reviewed. Check whether they are adequate to deal with racial (and sexual) harassment. Providing for an 'informal first stage', for example, can be an important way of encouraging workers to report harassment. Existing procedures can be amended or a special procedure agreed. A good procedure will:

- Set time limits – your member's right to take a case to Tribunal must not be put at risk. Remember, cases must be lodged within 3 months of the incident occurring.
- Provide for a short cut to the top – procedures must take account of circumstances where harassment has been carried out by a supervisor or middle manager.
- Guarantee complete confidentiality.
- Provide for union representation at all stages.
- Provide for special leave on full pay for your member, should s/he request it, pending the investigation.
- Provide for the alleged harasser to be sent home if there is a danger the harassment will be repeated.

* See Bruegel, *Feminist Review* No. 32.

© *Transport and General Workers' Union (TGWU)*

Blue-chip world shuts the door on ethnic minorities

A survey of some of Britain's biggest graduate recruiters has revealed that something is going badly wrong with so-called 'equal opportunities' policies. White applicants have almost twice as much chance of being selected as black or Asian candidates. John Izbicki reports.

When Susan Scott of the Commission for Racial Equality and Richard Kwiatkowski of the University of East London (UEL) wanted to find out just how well minority ethnic groups fared in the selection stakes, they approached 11 'blue-chip' companies, some of the biggest graduate recruiters in Britain. They were in for a shock.

The organisations all claimed to be 'committed to equal opportunities'. They included two large manufacturing companies, two of the big banks, two retail organisations, two finance firms and a large transport group.

The researchers fully expected to produce a 'best practice' study. To their surprise, they found that out of 55,832 applications made to these companies (6,500 from minority ethnic groups), white applicants stood almost twice as much chance of being selected as black or Asian candidates. Employers also seemed intent on re-inventing the line which had once divided polytechnics from universities. Graduates from 'new' universities, who possessed non-traditional qualifications, lower UCAS points scores or had re-sat A-levels to meet entry requirements, were practically doomed from the pre-selection stage.

There were three main hurdles to clear: the pre-selection stage, involving the sifting of application forms and letters; an interview; then a final assessment during which a variety of exercises and tests were taken over a period of one or two days.

Minority ethnic candidates were generally not disadvantaged by the interview stage. This in itself was also surprising, for if there was any thought of racial discrimination lingering in anyone's mind, it would have been expected to be at this stage. But the pre-selection and the final assessment stages proved the toughest of the obstacles for minority groups.

The researchers found that out of 55,832 applications made to these companies, white applicants stood almost twice as much chance of being selected as black or Asian candidates

---

Only one firm, which dealt with 10,300 candidates, decided to repeat the procedures three times, with each re-evaluation showing significant improvements in the treatment of minority groups. The first time, white candidates had almost six times more chance of succeeding than their black counterparts. The second time, this was reduced to a 2:1 chance and the third, it plummeted to an 'adverse impact ratio' of only 0.8.

When the researchers took a close look at the minority groups themselves, they found that candidates of Afro-Caribbean origin came bottom of the pile, being only half as likely to succeed in the pre-selection stage as those of Indian origin. Indians fared better than Bangladeshis, and Chinese graduates generally performed better than whites.

Another puzzling finding of this exhaustive piece of research, believed to be the first of its kind undertaken in Britain, was that selectors tended to take less notice of the class of degree obtained by applicants than of their O-level, GCSE and A-level grades. There was also evidence of mature applicants faring worse than those who went straight from school to university. Since many minority ethnic men and women tend to enter higher education later in life, first going to work, and perhaps bringing up a family before deciding on a university or college course, their chances of being selected were further reduced.

'It was quite clear that some employers had targeted Oxbridge and the Russell Group ("Ivy League") universities rather than the "new" universities,' said Mr Kwiatkowski, who is a senior lecturer in psychology at UEL. Overall, white applicants had 1.7 times more chance of being offered the job for which they applied than ethnic applicants. 'Of course, we were surprised,' said Mr Kwiatkowski. 'These companies represented the very best employers to co-operate with our study. They were all "blue chip" companies. Can you imagine what the worst employers might have turned out to be?'

Both Mr Kwiatkowski and Ms Scott ruled out deliberate direct discrimination. Instead, they suggested that cultural and other factors might operate to the disadvantage of certain groups of candidates. 'If a minority candidate at the interview stage expects to find bias or prejudice, he or she might alter their "normal" behaviour in all sorts of ways during

... SING THE SIXTH VERSE OF GOD SAVE THE QUEEN AND THE JOB IS YOURS...

SIMON FAIRBONE

the selection process. As a result, some of them might trip up,' said Mr Kwiatkowski.

He said that the data, which was presented to a conference of the British Psychological Society earlier this month, would now be examined more closely. It begs a number of important questions: what goes on in the minds of minority ethnic group applicants and their interviewers when they confront each other? And what is it that goes well for a black or Asian candidate in a first interview but badly at the final assessment stage?

Interviewers were changed all along the line, according to Mr Kwiatkowski. Pre-selection is conducted by one set of people, the interview by another – heads of department, line managers and the like – and the third, the final assessment, by yet another group of trained assessors.

'As far as assessment centres are concerned, we have very little to go on. There is an urgent need for further work to be done so that we can pinpoint the causes of the disparities this research has revealed,' he said.

© The Independent
January, 1998

Union equality

Do unions serve black workers?

The proportion of black workers in unions is falling faster than among whites. A Labour Research survey examines to what extent unions are addressing the issue of black participation.

The traditional image of unions is one dominated by white men. And that would convince anyone judging the movement by 'heads on the Tele'.

There is still only one black general secretary – Bill Morris of the T&G – and full-time officials are still predominantly white.

The TUC has to some extent tried to address that very public image of union leaders by, in 1994, establishing additional places on its top body, the general council, for members from ethnic minorities.

One of the current incumbents is Gloria Mills, director of equal opportunities in public services union UNISON. She said that the move was about ensuring there were black people at the heart of the movement's decision making and 'Making black workers visible and valued within the movement'.

She points to the change as one of three made within the TUC – the two others are the development of the annual black members' conference and the TUC Race Relations Committee – which have changed 'not only the agenda, but also the structure and culture of the TUC in favour of challenging and tackling race discrimination at large'.

However, her union, like most others, has not so far copied this tactic in its efforts to improve black members' representation. In fact a Labour Research survey of black and ethnic minority participation in 34 TUC-affiliated unions has found that only five have established reserved seats for black members on their ruling body.

Those that have are actors' union Equity, which has one council seat reserved for black and ethnic minority members, college lecturers' union NATFHE, which has two out of a total of 49, civil service union PTG, which has three out of 36, and the journalists', NUJ, which has one out of 18. In addition science and finance union MSF has places for two observers. The idea of reserved places was rejected by FDA black members after a 1990 consultation exercise.

The survey also found that little progress has been made by unions in the employment of black and ethnic minority full-time officials. Of the 31 unions providing information on this only nine employed any at all. UNISON has the most with 10 black regional officials, plus two out of eight new 'officer trainees' and a number of senior black specialists at its head office.

Some unions compensate for the lack of black officials to some extent by employing a specialist officer to deal with race equality issues. Only two in the survey – the NUT and UNISON – have an officer for whom that is their sole responsibility. But another 12 have a national officer with a more general equal rights remit.

But despite appearances at the top, the union movement is not an all-white bastion. It is true that unionisation is low among some ethnic groups – the proportion of Pakistani and Bangladeshi workers who are union members, for example, averages just 17% compared with 31% of white workers. But among black (African/Caribbean) workers 'union density', as this is known, is higher than for whites, at 36%.

But there are worrying signs of change here, as union density is declining more rapidly among black and other ethnic minority workers than among whites. Between 1995 and 1996, it fell by five percentage points for black employees compared with just one point for whites.

Among Pakistani/Bangladeshi men (not women) it also fell by five percentage points.

Individual unions have very little idea of how many members they have from ethnic minorities. Shopworkers' union USDAW has carried out research suggesting 4.7% of members are from ethnic minorities, while membership monitoring in the NUJ and the radiographers' union (SOR) both suggested a figure of 1.6%.

• The above is an extract from the BLINK (Black Information Link) web site which can be found at http://www.blsink.org.uk, produced by The 1990 Trust.

© The 1990 Trust

Staff fight to cure racism in the NHS

By Andrew Mullins

The Government has been accused of failing to tackle 'institutionalised racism' in the National Health Service, which is said to be blocking the careers of black and Asian doctors and nurses.

The first personnel strategy for Europe's largest employer, unveiled amid much fanfare last month by the Government, would do nothing to stamp out discrimination, according to equality campaigners. Racism found in British hospitals, they argue, is one of the main reasons for the chronic staff shortages in the NHS as the Department of Health battles against waiting lists. Some of the most talented black and Asian doctors find themselves trapped in the two grades immediately below consultant – two-thirds of all these doctors are from the ethnic minorities.

Dr Nizam Mamode, deputy chairman of the British Medical Association's junior doctors' committee, said: 'I've seen it again and again; there are very good surgeons who've come from India who know for a fact they will not be given a consultant's job in this country.

'It's out-and-out racism. It's a lot easier to deal with someone who speaks with a British accent than someone who doesn't; I think that's probably the distinguishing feature.'

The racism faced by the 'overseas' doctors is at its most obvious when they want to progress beyond the associate specialist or staff grades, of which they make up 65 per cent, to the next and highest grade – consultant – of which only 15 per cent are foreigners.

A Commission for Racial Equality report concluded: 'Black and Asian applicants were consistently less likely to be short-listed for, or appointed to, senior registrar or consultant posts than white applicants.'

But a source close to the Department of Health told The

Independent: 'I am very sceptical about whether the vast majority of [NHS] trusts are going to move seriously on race unless there is at least a threat of sanctions if they don't deliver.'

> **'I've seen it again and again; there are very good surgeons who've come from India who know for a fact they will not be given a consultant's job in this country'**

A report by Unison, the public service union, found that black Britons were put off from becoming nurses as a 'direct result' of the racism experienced by those nurses who arrived on the immigrant ship *Empire Windrush* 50 years ago.

The report also found 75 per cent of those black nurses already in the profession considered leaving the NHS last year. Roger Kline, national health secretary of the Manufacturing Science and Finance (MSF) union, which has 17,500 members who are nurses, said: 'The personnel strategy is too much of what you ought to do, rather than this is what you must do. Those [NHS hospital] trusts that are serious about doing something, will; those that aren't will hope it gets lost.

'The NHS is steeped in racism, so black staff are both leaving and not joining. The main reason is the sons and daughters of black nurses decide they don't want to experience the kind of treatment their parents have.'

Georgina English, NHS policy officer at the CRE, fears the human resources strategy may be as ineffective as the Programme of Action, a previous initiative. 'I have mentioned the Programme to senior people in NHS personnel and they were not aware of it,' she said.

Doctors' leaders believe racism can have a direct effect on the care of patients.

'Any discrimination breeds incompetence and incompetent people are getting through the system. This is clearly putting patients' safety at stake,' said Mr Mohib Khan, chairman of the British Medical Association's non-consultant career grade committee, which represents doctors who have finished their training but have not yet become consultants.

A survey carried out for the *British Medical Journal* found that ethnic minority doctors were six times more likely than white doctors to have complaints upheld against them by the Professional Conduct Committee of the General Medical Council.

Studies carried out by Dr Sam Everington and Dr Aneezh Esmail on racist attitudes in the medical profession, reported in the *British Medical Journal*, show a 'foreign' name is a handicap at every stage of a doctor's career.

In their articles, the two equality campaigners claimed that having an Asian surname reduced by half the likelihood of an interview for a junior doctor post as opposed to white applicants. They also claimed that white consultants were three times more likely to be rewarded financially through the merit award system.

Medical career 'shaped by bias'

Kai Sumana, 54, is a psychiatric nurse who says that the whole course of his career has been shaped by his battle against racism.

He came to the UK from Sierra Leone in 1964 when the National Health Service was advertising abroad for nurses because – like today – it was short of staff.

'I went into psychiatric nursing because I felt a black man would get on better there. Not many white people were keen to do psychiatry because of the stigma attached to mental illness. When I first arrived, I didn't realise I was being discriminated against, because I didn't know the culture.

'After a while I began to realise there was a lot of discrimination at work, in terms of promotion, in terms of allocation of responsibility.

'Even when you have the same capabilities and qualifications as white people, in the health service, black people are mostly overlooked for promotion,' Mr Sumana said.

In 1988 a new 'clinical' grading system was introduced for nurses, but Mr Sumana was not given the managerial 'G' grade he felt reflected the responsibility he had for running a ward. 'Unison fought very hard for me. We had to go all the way to Acas [Advisory, Conciliation and Arbitration Service] before I got the grade I really deserve,' he said.

It was a seven-year battle till Mr Sumana received the 'G' grade and £16,000 in back-pay. He now runs a psychiatric ward at night. A Unison report found that nursing staff from the ethnic minorities often believe they are more likely to have to work while their white colleagues sleep.

Student 'can fail just on colour'

Dr Nizam Mamode, 36, has a Mauritian father, although his mother is English and he was born in Britain, but he believes his name and the colour of his skin have exposed him to prejudice.

He encountered problems when applying for medical school. 'I had some difficulty getting in; at one point I had all the rejection slips pasted on my wall – it did make me wonder.'

Eventually he was accepted by St Andrews University to do his pre-clinical (first three years) training. Of the 20 exams he took, he got four first-class merit awards and 10 second-class. His clinical training was done at Glasgow University. 'There is clear evidence of discrimination in medical schools. Certain examiners are well known for failing black students, and sometimes do so. In a clinical exam it's much easier to give someone a hard time if you choose to.' He said he was aware of medical students in Britain who justifiably felt they were the victims of prejudice. Dr Mamode came across similar problems when he started work: 'There were episodes where I was aware of discriminatory attitudes on the ward. Someone would see my name on the roster and page me, when I turned up they would say, "Oh I expected someone who…" and then stop – meaning, "I was expecting someone darker, or with an accent".

'Since then I haven't had any problems with career progression; most people know me by now,' said Dr Mamode, who is deputy chairman of the BMA's junior doctor committee and a surgeon with a growing reputation at Glasgow Royal Infirmary.

© *The Independent*
October, 1998

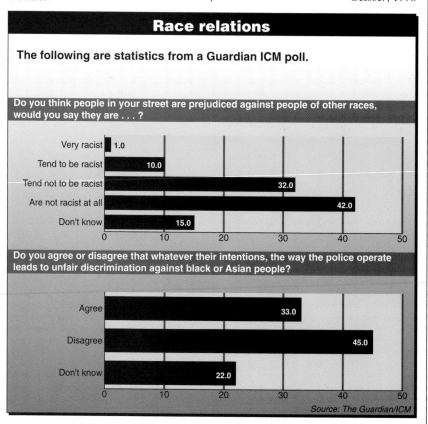

Race relations

The following are statistics from a Guardian ICM poll.

Do you think people in your street are prejudiced against people of other races, would you say they are . . . ?

Very racist	1.0
Tend to be racist	10.0
Tend not to be racist	32.0
Are not racist at all	42.0
Don't know	15.0

Do you agree or disagree that whatever their intentions, the way the police operate leads to unfair discrimination against black or Asian people?

Agree	33.0
Disagree	45.0
Don't know	22.0

Source: The Guardian/ICM

Military 'must wage war' on racism

Robertson considers US system to increase ethnic minority recruits. Gulf general says officers responsible for rooting out discrimination

---

By Richard Norton-Taylor

General Colin Powell, the black former chief of the US defence staff who rose to world notice during the Gulf war, yesterday called on Britain's armed forces to wage a crusade against racism and placed the responsibility for rooting it out squarely on the shoulders of senior officers.

Invited by George Robertson, the Defence Secretary, to help instil a culture of equal opportunities and eradicate racial harassment and discrimination in the military, General Powell told a Ministry of Defence conference in London: 'It is not policies or programmes which will get you to your goal, it will be the commanders and leaders who take this on as a central mission.'

In an unscripted, one-hour speech directed at an audience of military personnel, he described initiatives taken years ago in the US, but only now being adopted and considered in Britain.

They included special training sessions, zero tolerance campaigns, and close monitoring of the performance and attitudes of senior officers. 'In America, any overt expression of racism was absolutely crushed,' he said.

Mr Robertson referred to a passage in General Powell's autobiography: 'My career should serve as a model to fellow blacks, in or out of the military.' But while in the US blacks flocked to the armed forces to prove their worth, in Britain the problem was the reverse.

Only 1 per cent of Britain's sailors, soldiers, and airmen come from ethnic minorities which make up 6 per cent of the general population. They include just one Asian RAF group captain, one Asian Royal Navy commander, and three black and Asian colonels in the army.

An attempt to recruit more has been sabotaged by examples of racial harassment and abuse, readily acknowledged yesterday by General Sir Charles Guthrie, chief of the defence staff.

He called for a 'war on racism' and said there should be zero tolerance. However, as an example of how far Britain has to go to meet US standards, he said there was no formal reporting system assessing the record of officers and NCOs.

'My career should serve as a model to fellow blacks, in or out of the military'

Mr Robertson said later he was considering introducing a US-style system. 'We want to see armed forces which truly reflect our increasingly multi-cultural society and one in which women, as well as men, have every opportunity to progress.'

Sir Herman Ouseley, chairman of the Commission for Racial Equality, told the conference that two years ago he was in a 'state of war' with the Ministry of Defence. But progress had led to Sir Charles being presented with an award for promoting equal opportunities.

The task now, military sources say, is for the message to filter down to the barracks, messes, and parade ground.

The issue of gays and lesbians in the armed forces had proved 'very difficult' in the US, General Powell said earlier. The statutory 'don't ask, don't tell' policy, with gays and lesbians admitted to the armed forces so long as they kept their sexual orientation secret, had so far worked.

Mr Robertson said after the meeting that Britain's present ban – which is likely to be challenged by an expected European Court of Human Rights judgement – will be the subject of a free vote in the Commons before the end of this parliament.

© *The Guardian*
November, 1998

New plan to end racial harassment in the NHS

Targets to be set to reduce racial incidents

All NHS employers are to be set targets to reduce incidents of racial harassment as part of a major Government campaign to stamp out racism in the health service.

Speaking at the National Black Healthcare Forum in London Alan Milburn, the Health Minister, said that the zero tolerance campaign would challenge racial harassment of both staff and patients with perpetrators facing the threat of prosecution.

Mr Milburn was launching the new action plan 'Tackling racial harassment in the NHS' which he said was 'the most concerted drive the NHS has ever seen' on the issue.

The Plan quotes research from the Policy Studies Institute (PSI) about the prevalence of racial harassment inside the health service. The research showed that:

- 66 per cent of black nursing staff said they had difficulties with patients for ethnic reasons.
- 58 per cent of Asian nursing staff said they had difficulties with patients for ethnic reasons.
- 37 per cent of black nursing staff said they had difficulties with colleagues for ethnic reasons.
- 37 per cent of Asian nursing staff said they had difficulties with colleagues for ethnic reasons.

It says that harassment takes a number of forms and that it has become accepted almost as part of the job by many black and ethnic minority staff.

The Plan says that by April 2000 every NHS employer will need to be in position to tackle racial harassment whether committed by staff or by patients. Progress will be measured. Targets for reducing incidents will be set.

A major public awareness campaign targeted at staff and patients alike will highlight the impact of racial harassment and the fact that it will not be tolerated in any NHS setting.

Black and ethnic minority staff will be given support to change harassment effectively.

Perpetrators of racial harassment will be challenged. Persistent perpetrators will face prosecution.

Mr Milburn said: 'The launch of this action plan signals the Government's intent to ensure that there is zero tolerance of racism in every part of the NHS.

'Racial harassment and discrimination cannot be tolerated in a service that rightly prides itself on its intrinsic fairness. It is simply unacceptable for people who come to work to care for others to put up with discrimination and prejudice whether from patients, visitors or other staff.

'The NHS relies on its black and ethnic minority staff. Without them the health service would cease to function.

'As the biggest employer of black and ethnic minority staff in the country I am determined that the NHS will set an example of others to follow.'

A national strategic group will steer this service-wide programme to tackle racial harassment building on the Government's efforts over the last eighteen months to deal with racism in the NHS.

We have signed the NHS up to the CRE's Leadership Challenge and launched the NHS Equality Awards to celebrate the achievements the NHS has made in equal opportunities.

We have increased the representation of people from ethnic minorities appointed to NHS Trust and Health Authority boards. Since 1 May 1997, 10 per cent of all Trust and Health Authority board appointees have been from an ethnic minority background (comparing with 5 per cent before this date and 6 per cent ethnic minority population in the UK as a whole).

We have changed the doctors' distinction awards system to help eradicate racial bias and ensure that awards are genuinely made on ground of merit and merit alone.

We have told NHS employers that they need to show progress towards a workforce that year on year becomes more representative of the community it serves.

© Crown Copyright, 1998

What's it all about?

The facts, views and tales of racism in football

It's sometimes hard to believe there's still racism in football. After all, football is for everyone isn't it? But unfortunately it's true.

Only recently West Ham's Eyal Berkovic complained of anti-Jewish racism on the pitch from Blackburn players; and Leicester fans reported racist chanting from Leeds supporters when the teams met at Filbert Street. Incidents like these, and the others we highlight on this page, are rarer than they used to be, but even one is too many.

We know black faces are common on the pitch, but where are they in the crowd, why are there so few black managers or coaches, why are there no black chairmen or directors? And where are the Asians in football? Something's got to be wrong here.

That's what this information is all about. If football is for everyone then we have to rid the game of racism. And that's where you come in. Young people are the future of the game, as fans, players, or as future bosses of the FA. If young people are taking the lead on these issues then the future of the beautiful game is secure.

After all, football is for everyone.

The facts

Only about 1% of fans who go to football matches come from ethnic minority groups.

Professional players in Holland once went on strike to protest against racism in the game. Players have campaigned in Italy, Germany and Britain too.

It is said that 25% of professional players are black, but this number is diminishing, partly because of the number of foreign imports in the game.

The number of black players in youth schemes is now only about 7%.

The percentage of black pros playing in the top flight has fallen from around 50% to about 33% in the last five years.

On average, only 32 people are successfully prosecuted for racist chanting or abuse each year in the whole country.

Kick this out

Racist abuse in English football does still happen. These are from 1997 alone:

Nov 1997
Dwight Yorke has racist abuse shouted at him throughout Aston Villa's UEFA Cup game in Bucharest – then he scores

Nov 1997
Chester manager Kevin Ratcliffe has to pay James Hussaney £2,500 damages for racially insulting the Chester apprentice in training but he is cleared of racial discrimination for releasing him from the club

Oct 1997
Chelsea boss Ruud Gullit is called 'nigger' by Bolton fans while warming up as substitute at the Reebok Stadium

Oct 1997
An armed mob shout racial abuse and assault members of a mainly-black amateur team in Leeds. They chases the players with knives, bats, bottles, a sword and a hammer

Oct 1997
Sol Campbell is abused by Italian fans before and during England's draw in Rome

Sept 1997
PFA investigate allegations that Warren Aspinall (now Brentford) made monkey gestures at Plymouth's Ronnie Mauge while playing for Carlisle

Sept 1997
At Elland Road, Leeds fans target abuse at Leicester and England Under-21 striker Emile Heskey and sing anti-Asian songs at Leicester fans

May 1997
Stephen Roberts, a black 20-year-old amateur player, is kicked in the head and called a 'black b******' after scoring the winner in a Cup Final in Glasgow

March 1997
Nathan Blake refuses to play for Wales after accusing Bobby Gould of racist remarks in training

Out of Africa

When England play Tunisia in the World Cup this summer, Exeter striker Sufyan Ghazghazi will have split loyalties. His Dad is Tunisian, but he was born and brought up in Devon and played for England schoolboys. As one of very few English-born players of African descent to make it through the system into the pro game, Sufyan knows what it feels like to 'be different'.

'I've always had minor taunts from people but nothing really bad,' says the 20-year-old forward. 'There are not many black people in Devon – we were the only family at our school – but I think that made it easier for me. We were something different and people gave us a go, without pre-judging us. I think it's harder for blacks or Asians in somewhere like London, where people have already made their minds up about whole races. Kids hear their parents shout racist abuse and copy them. But the kids around here grew up with me and treat me well. There are still little things, but I think racism has improved over the years.'

What the stars think . . .

Rio Ferdinand, West Ham and England

There have been big improvements but there is still racism. I haven't experienced any myself but I heard opposition players get abuse and I've wanted to say that I know how they feel. We're unlikely to get it among team-mates at West Ham because we have a lot of black players. That can only help as our fans idolise us – black or white – and see us mixing on and off the field. They should take that into consideration in their own lives.

Gareth Southgate, Aston Villa and England

I was disgusted by the reaction some opposition crowds gave our black players at Crystal Palace. But we showed our loyalty to our team-mates and tried to impress on them that not everybody feels that way. We train, play and socialise together and we are from different races. Hopefully that's a symbol to the fans that there's harmony on the field and let's have it off the field as well.

Danny Cadamarteri, Everton and England youth

I knew that few black players had ever joined Everton and what other people said about the club went through my mind before joining. But I haven't experienced any racism either at Everton or away grounds. I did get some sly comments in Sunday football and it made me mad that people could be so ignorant. But if they were, they're not worth bothering with. They won't put me off my game. Young people of different races mix together from an early age so racist comments are more likely to come from their parents. Most youngsters realise it's the person who's important, not the colour of their skin.

Paul Ince, Liverpool and England

I could be walking down the street with my wife Clare, who's white, and nine out of ten people would say, 'There's Paul Ince with his wife'. But if I was a normal black guy, they'd say, 'Look at that black bloke with a white girl'. That can't be right. Sometimes people are jealous of black and Asian people for what they've achieved since coming over here. Some white people still look down on blacks like they have ever since we were slaves.

© Kick It Out

Racism in football

Information from the Football Association (FA)

Football is the world game, played in every nation by every race, colour and creed. But the game in this country has also played host to some of the worst racist abuse, aimed at black players on the pitch.

A history of black footballers

Players of African and Caribbean origin have a long history in the English game. The first black professional was Arthur Wharton, a goalkeeper for the Preston North End team in the 1880s which won the Football League in its first two seasons (1888-90). Wharton's grave was discovered recently in South Yorkshire, and he is now properly commemorated as an early football hero, after a campaign by local fans.

Other notable pioneers include William Tull, who played for Spurs before World War I. Albert Johannson, a South African, was the first black player to appear in an FA Cup Final, with Leeds United in 1965. The late 1960s and early 70s saw a big increase in black players, many of whom arrived in Britain from the Caribbean.

By 1978 there were 50 black professionals, including the trio of Cyrille Regis, Laurie Cunningham and Brendan Batson in the successful West Bromwich Albion team. Viv Anderson became the first black player to represent England, in a game against Czechoslovakia at Wembley on 29 November 1978, and went on to win 30 caps.

Now an estimated 25% of professional players are black, and many have gone on to achieve great success, as international players (Paul Ince became the first black England captain against USA in 1993) or in other fields (Brendon Batson is now Deputy Chief Executive of the Professional Footballers' Association, and Garth Crooks is a well-known sports broadcaster).

Let's kick racism out of football

From the 1970s, black players were often subject to virulent racial abuse from the terraces, with few attempts at combating it. In the 1993/94 season, the Professional Footballers' Association and the Commission for Racial Equality (CRE) came together to launch the 'Let's Kick Racism Out of Football' campaign with the aim of ensuring that all those who go to see the game can do so without fear of racial abuse or harassment.

The campaign focused its attention initially on professional clubs; contacts were made and an action plan produced (see below), which focused on specific measures each club could take to both clamp down on racist abuse and encourage a more positive attitude towards ethnic minorities.

In its second season, 91 professional clubs signed up to the campaign, and further support came from the Football Trust, the Football Supporters' Association (FSA) and the National Federation of Football Supporters' Clubs (NFFSC). Surveys showed that increasing numbers of fans were becoming aware of the campaign, and many clubs were now taking active steps to combat racism at their grounds.

10-point action plan for football clubs

1. Make, and display, a statement saying that a club will not tolerate racism, and will take specific action against supporters who engage in racial abuse, chanting or intimidation.

2. Make public announcements condemning racist chanting at matches, and warning that the club will not hesitate to take action.

3. Make it a condition for season-ticket holders that they do not take part in racist abuse, chanting or any other offensive behaviour.

4. Take action to prevent the sale or distribution of racist literature in and around grounds.

5. Take disciplinary action against players who racially abuse players, officials and supporters before, during and after matches.

6. Contact other clubs to make sure they understand the club's policy on racism.

7. Make sure that stewards and the police understand the club's policy and have a common strategy for handling abusive supporters. If it is dangerous to take action against offenders during the match, they should be identified and barred from future games.

8. Remove all racist graffiti from grounds as a matter of urgency.

9. Adopt an equal opportunities policy.

10. Work with others to develop pro-active programmes and projects to raise awareness of the campaign and institute action to eliminate racist abuse.

Examples: Charlton Athletic
The club and its supporters launched Red White & Black at the Valley, a partnership with the local council, police and racial equality council. This included leaflets, posters, messages in match programmes,

tannoy announcements and visits by players to local schools and community groups. The campaign has focused on encouraging more fans from ethnic minority communities and has received funding of £500,000 from local government.

Leyton Orient
A number of initiatives by the Community Development scheme have been developed, the most successful being an anti-racist play, called *Kicking Out*, which brought the issues of racism to a young audience in an entertaining and informative way. Such was the success of the play that it went nation-wide, and was seen by more than 100,000 people.

Football unites against racism
After the success of the campaign in its first two years in highlighting the continuing problems of racism, a major step forward was taken in 1995/96 when The Football Association joined the existing partners in bringing together representatives of all areas of the game to form the Advisory Group Against Racism & Intimidation (AGARI).

This was the first time that all strands of opinion in football – players, managers, fans, match officials and the authorities – had come together in a common cause.

'The situation there (in Italy) is like it was years ago in England, with monkey chanting and the like. In England we've made a stand against racism and people appreciate that it has to be stamped out.' (Paul Ince).

AGARI expanded the activities of 'Let's Kick Racism Out of Football', holding a series of high profile events, often involving football stars such as Ruud Gullit and John Barnes, and working closely with many clubs to promote the campaign.

The campaign also focused on particular issues as they arose: after severe racial abuse directed at black Arsenal players in a match at Barnsley, the club were encouraged to take action against fans and subsequently raised the profile of their own anti-racism campaign.

Members of the campaign
The Football Association, FA Premier League, Professional Footballers' Association, Football Trust Commission for Racial Equality, League Managers' Association, Football Supporters' Association, National Federation of Football Supporters' Clubs, Association of Premier and Football League Match Officials, The Football Conference Football Safety Officers' Association, Local Government Association, Metropolitan Police.

'It's important that fans know that we're not prepared to tolerate racism. The more people stand up and be counted about it, the more people's attitudes will change.' (Graeme le Saux).

Local initiatives
The national campaign has inspired a number of local groups to campaign against racism in their local areas.

Show Racism the Red Card
Established in Newcastle by Youth Against Racism in Europe, the local campaign has, through the active involvement of footballers such as Shaka Hislop and Les Ferdinand, reached many schoolchildren through a video and visits. The video was so successful that a new version on a European theme has been produced, involving interviews with English and foreign football stars.

Football Unites – Racism Divides
Sheffield football supporters came together with Sheffield United FC, the police, local community and youth organisations and members of black communities to address local problems with racist behaviour, and encourage greater ethnic minority involvement in football. Local youths were involved in footballing training sessions and community forums, and new policing strategies for match days established around the football club.

Hounslow Grassroots Anti-racism Initiative
Hounslow Council in West London launched an initiative to take the 'Let's Kick Racism Out of Football' campaign into grassroots football, played on council-owned pitches. Local leagues have signed a declaration against racism, which is now displayed in all dressing rooms in the area.

Kick It Out – the new campaign

The latest development in the Let's Kick Racism Out of Football campaign has been the establishing of an independent organisation called Kick It Out (KIO). With financial backing from the FA, PFA, Premier League and Football Trust, Campaign Co-ordinators have been appointed to work with the member organisations, and develop new campaigns. The key areas of focus for the campaign are to: continue the work with clubs at the professional football level, combat racism in grassroots football through work with local partners, take the campaign into Europe and the World Cup and increase ethnic minority participation in all areas of the game.

There is no doubt that progress has been made in combating racism in football, and football can be proud of the lead it has given to other sports and society as a whole.

For further information about the Let's Kick Racism Out of Football campaign, please contact KIO at Business Design Centre, 52 Upper Street, London N1 0QH, Tel: 0171 288 6012. E-mail: kick-racism@kick-it-out.demon.co.uk.

Suggested reading

Williams, J. *'Lick my boots . . . '* *Racism in English Football*, Sir Norman Chester Centre for Football Research, Leicester University (1992)
Woolnough, B. *Black Magic: England's Black Footballers*, London (1983)
Hill, D. *Out of His Skin: The John Barnes Phenomenon*, Faber (1989)
KIO Office, *Kicking Out Magazines*. (1997)

© Football Association (FA)

Racism in football

Danny & Dale

When you are at a football game, there are usually three different types of people:
1. The know-it-alls who think the manager is always wrong.
2. The quiet people that never say anything.
3. The racist.

And it's the racists that discourage other races from getting involved in football.

Asians in football

Asians for example aren't usually associated with football, but a Manchester University study in 1991 found that a higher proportion of people from Asian communities play football, than any others, including domestic whites. For example, 60% of Bengalis compared to 47% of white people.

Jas Bains is a director of the project 'Asians can't play football', set up last year in the Midlands to find out why the target of playing at a professional level has remained out of range for Asians.

He outlines the common excuses: 'According to myth, Asians are either not interested in football, not strong enough for a contact sport or not competitive enough for the top levels.

'It's said that they won't make it because their parents will want them to go into the family business or they won't have time for training because they'll need to go to the mosque. But it's rubbish. There's no scientific evidence to say Asians are physically weaker. And no one who has seen Asians play cricket, hockey or kabbadi can say we lack competitive edge.'

Fans go bananas

Thankfully the indiscriminate racism on the terraces of the 80s has, to some extent, diminished.

John Barnes, the Charlton midfielder, recalls that in 1985 he was a target of abuse from fans sharing a plane on the way to a World Cup warm-up tournament in Mexico.

Also, when he moved from Watford to Liverpool, bananas were thrown at him during derby matches involving Everton. More recently, West Ham striker Ian Wright has been involved in a number of controversial incidents.

In January 1995, he was criticised on the eve of his team's FA Cup game against Millwall at the New Den. The player said he hated playing there because supporters were racially abusive.

Nike shows the way

Even though racism is still happening, things are being done to stop it.

Nike the sportswear multinational transmitted a television commercial featuring Eric Cantona speaking out against racism in football.

The 30-second black and white ad, which also features the black Tottenham and England striker, Les Ferdinand, was televised on the 24th March 1995.

It shows both men playing football and saying they want to get on with the game irrespective of their race or nationality. The ad was transmitted in France and was supported by the country's Commission of Racial Equality as part of its 'Kick Racism out of Football' campaign.

The battle to stop racism is far from over, but we hope it soon will be, for football's sake!

© Haringey Youth Online

Andy Cole talks exclusively to Kick It Out!

England ace Andy Cole talks to Nick Varley

Have you experienced racism, not just in football, but in life in general?
You do experience it generally. For me personally, it was a lot harder when I was younger. Now it's just like water off a duck's back. I know how to handle it much better.

Is there any one incident in football which sticks in your mind?
When I was a teenager looking to join a club I was at one ground and a certain player came up to me and goes, 'Are you alright chalkie?', which just set my mind against that club there and then, and I just decided I wouldn't be signing for them. To be honest, it would have been better for me personally if I'd signed for that club at that time, but that incident changed my mind totally and I went to Arsenal instead. I never had any trouble at all at Arsenal. There were a lot of black pros in the team at the time – Paul Davis, Michael Thomas, David Rocastle – people like that – so it was better for me.

What about when you became a first-team player?
I got none whatsoever at Bristol City and that was a really good thing, because I'd heard of it going on there and at certain places where we played. Obviously, before I went to Newcastle I'd heard all about the racist abuse there but I had no problems. At one stage my family came up and had a bit of stick, but personally I had no trouble.

What happened with your family?
They came up to a game one day and suffered a bit of racist abuse outside the ground. I was really disappointed for my family to experience that because I'd been up there for so long without any problems. I thought it was bang out of order. They were coming up to support me, like a lot of other fans, and they got that.

Do you think the situation is getting better or worse?
It's definitely getting a lot better – but there's still a lot to do. There's a big change from 20 years ago or whatever. A lot of my friends, who are a bit older, come to games now and they say years ago they couldn't even have come. But there is still a lot of racism and it's not settled.

Have you ever talked to any of the older players about how bad it used to be?
Speaking to some of the black players now who've been around a bit longer than me they say it's a lot better than it was before, when they first started. I think it is a lot easier now for black players to play football in whatever division because most people look at us differently now. At one stage you'd be stereotyped – you know, 'They don't like it when the weather's cold', and stuff like that. I think that's all changed now. I hope people look at a black player, who's a good player, and just say, 'He's a good player'.

Do you get more racism abroad?
Yeah, last season at Juventus. I got quite a lot there, and a little bit this season against Feyenoord. But that was it, just those two games.

And what about in the stands?
Well some people don't want to speak out because they don't want to get involved, but those who do will be the ones who get things moving. Then other people sitting next to them will say, 'I don't want to hear that sort of thing, either', and they can get them ejected.

That's where it's going to stop. Only when people themselves make a stand and say, 'I'm not having that'. Sometimes you will have to stand up against your brother, sister, Mum or Dad and show them your beliefs.

Attitudes to racial chanting by age

The survey categorised supporters into three groups regarding their attitudes to racism. Supporters' responses were split into the following order: accept, mixed, dislike. Elderly supporters showed their opposition with 82 per cent against racist comments.

Age	Accept	Mixed views	Dislike	Total	Sample size
Less than 20	23	13	64	100	143
20-39	22	11	67	100	492
40-59	15	10	75	100	415
60 and over	10	8	82	100	146
Total	18	10	72	100	1196

Source: The Survey and Statistical Research Centre, Sheffield Hallam University/Football Unites – Racism Divides (FURD)

At the end of the day, it doesn't matter how racist you are, you will know in yourself that it's wrong to hate someone because of the colour of their skin.

How does it affect you?
You don't let it. They're just mindless bigots. If that's the way they want to go about things then it's up to them. But if you let it affect you then they've won.

What about when you were younger or when it happened to your parents?
Sometimes it affected me worse than others – it depended what mood I was in. It still does really. Sometimes I lose my temper and sometimes it's just nothing.

Sometimes you can handle it and sometimes you just don't want to handle it, you've had enough of it.

Is it different if someone makes a comment off the pitch, when you can see the person saying it?
Yeah. I find that a lot harder. I find that just disrespectful. On the pitch or from the crowd during a game it could be in the heat of the moment or whatever. But off the pitch when people have time to think about what they're saying that's when I have a problem. That's the time when I might lose my temper.

Has racism ever made you think about giving up football?
No. Again, for you to be considering retiring from the game or not playing because a few people are saying

certain things that means you're weak and I refuse to be put down by people like that.

Do you think it makes a difference that there are so many foreign players in the premiership now?
At Manchester United we've every nationality and that helps I'm sure. But when it comes to black people at lower levels or in other walks of life, everyone handles it in different ways. Some people might not like me because of the colour of my skin, but they like what I do. I do know though how I'd go about it if I wasn't a professional footballer. I don't think I'd be so diplomatic.

Is that why you're involved in this campaign?
That's right, because it's a way of saying things. By speaking out publicly, I hope it helps.

What can fans do to stop racism?
If someone's sitting next to someone who says something racist and they let it go, there's like a domino effect. Someone else will think it's OK to say something racist and so on. If they say stop then that domino effect stops.

Do you have any message on racism for your fans or any younger fans who look up to you?
If you want to look at me as a role model, look at the way I conduct myself – at the highest level. I had knockbacks when I was younger, but you've got to deal with them as best

you can. You've got to decide what you'll accept and what you won't and it's a thin line – and it's very hard. It's always still in the back of my mind though, because I've got a little boy now and I wouldn't want him to grow up and have to experience what I did because it's not nice. I don't think it's right.

Watch the stars speak out
Show racism the red card, a new video featuring action and interviews with nearly fifty top Premiership and international players. Stars like Ryan Giggs, Les Ferdinand, Steve McManaman and Gianfranco Zola speak out against racism and tell fans how to give racism the red card.

Here's what Man United hero Ryan Giggs, whose father is black, has to say about his experiences: 'You come across the odd bit of racism both in primary and secondary school. It's similar to bullying. I mean, as a kid it affects your whole life, so it's not very nice when it's happening to you. Talk to someone. Teachers, maybe parents, can help you because, as I say, it can affect your school work, affect your life and make it a misery.'

• The video lasts 30 minutes and is perfect to show school classes. To buy a copy, send a cheque for £55 (inc p&p) to 'Show Racism The Red Card', 1 Drury Lane, Newcastle-upon-Tyne, NE1 1EA. (Includes education pack, study notes and magazine.)
© Andrew Cole Enterprises Ltd

Anti-racism and football

A new direction?

The racist abuse of black players and black and ethnic minority fans alike has been a consistent aspect of the British game in and around football grounds throughout the game's history but especially over the past thirty years. It has often provided an intimidating and offensive environment for black people and has arguably stifled the development of the game by restricting the influx of talented black and

Asian players into the British game and, by tarnishing the image of football, ultimately affecting the commercial attractiveness of the game for potential sponsors.

However, a number of factors have contributed to what, in the 1990s, is an excellent opportunity to oppose racism in the football environment. The pioneering role of black players of the 1970s has provided the impetus and the role

models for the young emerging black talent which now leads the way in both Premiership football, and at international level. Paul Ince recently became the first black player to captain England. The new manager of the England Women's team is a black female, Hope Powell. Around one in six professional male footballers in England are black, whilst fewer than one in a hundred supporters are black, and the CRE/

PFA campaign hopes to redress this imbalance by making football grounds a much more 'civilised' environment. Asian spectators are also vastly under-represented at matches, especially in light of the fact that many grounds are located amid large Asian communities. The post-Hillsborough shift in terrace culture and the associated changes in the general behaviour of fans also provide a potentially promising basis for the future of black and Asian involvement in the British game.

While blacks have fought through prejudice to excel at the highest levels of English football, we still await the Asian 'breakthrough'. As of 1997-98, there are no Asian professionals in England. Many people within the game offer up tired stereotypes as explanations: 'their builds are too slight to take the physical abuse'. Jas Bains in *Asians Can't Play Football* seeks to address the reasons for the lack of Asian representation in professional football. His findings are illuminating: football is extremely popular among young British males of Asian origin, many aspire to play professionally, and most feel that the lack of Asians in professional football is due to lack of opportunity. Further findings expose the ignorance and racism of the football establishment: 55% of club officials surveyed thought that football was 'not popular' among British Asians, 69% thought that Asian footballers were physically inferior to those from other groups, and 86% thought they were either definitely or possibly less talented than players drawn from other groups. 65% of Asian footballers claimed to have regularly suffered racist abuse while playing organised football. As a result of racism Asians often play on segregated sides and in segregated leagues; leagues which professional clubs do not scout.

From the inception of the anti-racism movement in football in the 1980s, it has generally targeted the far-right, neo-Nazi skinhead groups – and justifiably so. But now that

this type of violent, overtly racist activity has been drastically reduced, anti-racist efforts must not simply slow down. Back, Crabbe, and Solomos (1996) warn against the perception, perpetuated by the media, that all racist activity within the game is personified in the 'skinhead Nazi'. Such a 'narrow emphasis on fan behaviour and an out of date image allow more subtle forms of racism to go unchallenged' (*When Saturday Comes*, November 1997). They condemn the 'Blind Eye Syndrome' – wherein 'racist name-calling or playful racial insults' at football matches are seen as acceptable because the perpetrators are 'normal people', not neo-Nazis. Such 'every-day racism' is pervasive and even widely accepted, seen by fans as no more harmful than taunting a player because he is bald or overweight. Television commentators have been guilty of avoiding the unpleasant subject of racism. Racist chanting and abuse has been lightly dismissed as part of the 'electric atmosphere', or condoned as merely the crowd 'getting on' the player, but for the most part ignored entirely (Back, et al 1996).

Back, et al. (1996), also see institutional racism as a strong force in football today, commenting that it is: 'easy for everyone to support a campaign against racism in football when it is targeted against patho-logically aggressive, neo-Nazi thugs. It might prove a little more tricky to generate football-wide support if we were to start asking questions about

the attitudes in the board-room, on the pitch, and in the training ground.' Black managers are rare, as are black club officials, or even club employees. Wide-spread racist stereotypes about blacks abound among the nearly all-white club managers, coaches, administrators and offic-ials, particularly that they are athletically gifted but intellectually inferior. Within this racist culture, blacks do not make suitable managers or coaches. Asians are seen as physically and athletically inferior, lacking the robust physique as well as the skill needed to play professional football in Britain. Breaking down the persistent institutional racism within the game will be a tremendous challenge, perhaps more difficult than reducing the hooliganism and neo-Nazi racist activity prevalent in the 1970s and 1980s.

The 1990s present, potentially at least, the opportunity for a new era within British football. The restructuring of the game, a massive ground improvement programme, a revitalised commercial interest in the game, rising attendance and the general improvement in fan behaviour has placed football firmly back in its place as a central part of the cultural fabric of the nation. Within the national sport black and Asian participation is not only to be welcomed; it is absolutely necessary for the future of the national game. This is not to mention the wider social benefits of a sport which accommodates black and Asian spectators and players. The way forward is succinctly outlined by the CRE/PFA campaign which states that:

'If football is to be played and enjoyed equally by everyone, what-ever the colour of their skin, and wherever they come from, it is up to us all, each and every one of us, to refuse to tolerate racist attitudes, and to demand nothing less than the highest standards in every area of the game.'

© Sir Norman Chester
Centre for Football Research

FA launch biggest ever footy racism crackdown

New guidelines make racism at matches a criminal offence for everyone, including players and referees. By Eva Simpson

The biggest ever crackdown on racism in football has been launched by the government.

This week, the Football Task Force, chaired by ex-MP David Mellor, declared war on those who would besmirch the 'beautiful game' with bigotry.

The new moves mean:

- A red card and fine for any player racially abusing another;
- A new criminal offence of racist chanting by individual spectators;
- Putting an anti-racism clause into the contracts of players and managers; .
- Hiring more black and Asian coaches, as well as referees and
- Encouraging clubs to adopt equal opportunity policies.

The Task Force, set up by Sports Minister Tony Banks last July, has taken evidence from around the country.

It has found that while many black players are seen at the pinnacle of the game, there were not enough ethnic minorities working behind the scenes.

And the lower down football's pecking order you go, the worse the racism can get.

Within the last month alone a footballer with 'The Islanders', who play in the Corinthian League in east London, was poked in the face with a machete by an opponent and Leeds-based GN Khalsa have been given police protection for matches.

Their problems in the Sunday League began when they thrashed opponents in the racist east end of the city 9-0.

A gang of thugs invaded the pitch wielding samurai swords, knives and baseball bats.

Luckily no one was injured in the attack. But a few weeks later the mob launched a similar assault on the older A team in which they threatened to return with 'tools'.

Angry team boss Joe Bravo who has been in charge of the club for nearly 20 years told *Caribbean Times*: 'We had a meeting with police and threatened to take things into our own hands as a result they have been escorting us to all our home games.

While many black players are seen at the pinnacle of the game, there are not enough ethnic minorities working behind the scenes

---

'The people you are dealing with are thugs and druggies and they don't make idle threats. That's why it's very necessary to have protection.'

Local community liaison officer Insp Kevin Spencer said: 'The incidents were very nasty and clearly racially motivated and there was a lot of criticism about the way the police responded.

'Now we are ensuring a police presence so we can make arrests if anything happens.'

The Task Force plans to deal with such incidents through broadening the 'Hounslow Initiative' under which clubs, leagues and county FAs sign anti-racist declarations which appear on all council pitches.

Failure to comply would mean automatic exclusion from the league in question.

It is hoped that such measures will encourage more black and Asian youngsters into parks football.

© Caribbean Times
April, 1998

Percentage of non-white fans

Club	%
Leeds United	1.1%
Blackburn Rovers	0.9%
Southampton	0.7%
Nottingham Forest	0.7%
Everton	0.7%
Derby County	0.6%
Middlesborough	0.5%
Sheffield Wednesday	0.4%
Glasgow Rangers	0.3%
Newcastle	0.2%
Sunderland	0.1%

Club	%
Arsenal	4.1%
Manchester United	2.1%
Leicester	2.0%
Tottenham	1.9%
Wimbledon	1.7%
Coventry City	1.6%
Liverpool	1.4%
Chelsea	1.1%
Aston Villa	1.1%
West Ham	1.1%

Source: 1997 Premier League Fan Survey

Soccer's hidden racism: blowing the whistle

Are anti-racist football campaigns reaching the grassroots?

Anti-racism has now, partly because of high-profile efforts from the CRE and its chairman Sir Herman Ouseley, made its way into football. This year's Kick It Out campaign, backed by Blair and Hoddle, was launched in January with the Home Secretary visiting Birmingham City Football Club, and Tony Banks was guest speaker at a conference organised by socialist MEPs at Old Trafford on 'Tackling racism in football across Europe'.

Increasingly, those who want to influence young people are using well-known footballers to spread the anti-racist word. In Scotland, Hearts striker Jose Quintongo and Hibernian's defender Algerian Jean-Marc Boco recently launched Edinburgh's poster campaign to reinforce zero tolerance of racism.

It was, of course, a massive step forward. Only six years ago it was left to a handful of dedicated radicals in supporters' groups to raise the issue of racism. It was local community campaigners leafleting against fascists and racists on the terraces. While black players and supporters got abused, no one in the board rooms seemed to care. The high-profile campaigning has begun to change things. A commitment to anti-racism is now expected of the top clubs, so much so that Wimbledon's failure to support the local Kick It Out action group by 27 January became newsworthy. And even David Mellor, head of the government's Football Task Force, was prepared to stick his neck out to defend a sacked black manager.

But now that anti-racism in football has impetus, it must go beyond exhortations from key spokesmen and campaigns that involve only Premier League stars. It must begin to trickle down to affect the running of the game all the way through. There are indications that anti-racism in football might dissipate its initiative in empty, politically correct gesture politics. Why, for example, was there such a concerted attack on BBC commentator John Motson for a chance remark, when someone like Jimmy Greaves was for years allowed to get away with the most outrageous comments on prime-time TV?

Racism in local league football

At the other end of football's spectrum, in local leagues, sportsmen are being driven out of the game by racism, and clubs with 'too many' black players are being discriminated against. Terry Dannie of Gillingham talked to CARF about his experience. He loves football, which he has played since he was 12. Today,

at 29, he is outraged that he now faces a ban for life because he was sent off in five games in a row. 'When I take a free kick, I get called all sorts things like "black bastard". We get abuse from other teams all the time.' When he and other team-mates reacted to racist abuse, they got shown the red card. Terry feels the way he and the other black players are singled out is totally unfair.

'Nothing ever happens to the other side,' he says bitterly about the racist taunters. The manager of the Boatswain and Call pub side is considering withdrawing the team from the league because the young side, eight of whom are black, are 'fed up with how they are treated'. The Rochester District League's spokesman says that a written warning about racism has gone to all clubs and refs. If that is so, it has had little effect.

Where can Terry go from here? We asked the Kick It Out campaign. They admitted that they get letters from players like Terry every day but, unfortunately, with 3,500 clubs in their remit (and only two workers) they just can't take up individual cases. They have also found that intervening on a player's behalf with a local FA can even exacerbate a racism problem and penalise players yet further.

Entrenched views

Entrenched views in local FAs are something Leeds Road TRA football club in Huddersfield know all about. This all-black team, in an all-white local FA, has been fighting a two-month ban which would have dashed all hopes of promotion and cup glory. (The team has been reinstated after an appeal but the fine levied on the club has not been returned.) The West Riding County FA had taken harsh punitive action against it after an incident last November involving a supporter who quarrelled with a referee. Roy Akins, Leeds Road's manager, explains: 'Referees think we are aggressive because we are black,' while striker Kirk Smith insists that black players get worse treatment than whites. Akins is cynical about the FA's backing for the Kick It Out campaign. For him the issue is more than mere abuse from supporters: 'It's about who runs the game and takes all the decisions.'

Local initiatives

National campaigns may not be directly affecting entrenched attitudes at local level. But there are nonetheless a plethora of new initiatives at the grass-roots which might enable anti-racism to 'trickle up'. For example, the anti-racist play

Ooh, Ah Showab Khan, about the battle of an Asian player to get into the Premier League, written by a Barking-based drama company and premiered in Newham last year, is now touring thousands of schools all over Britain. And in February Camden United, a youth team of Asian, African-Caribbean and white European players created in 1995 to defuse racial tensions in Somers Town, played Celtic Rangers from Ireland. This team, a non-sectarian squad, brings together Protestant and Catholic players from Dublin and Belfast.

In many schools teachers have been encouraging pupils to support the call to kick racism out of football. Primary school children have been creating their own anti-racist posters for a national competition. In Gloucestershire the Stroud Poets have, with Brockworth school, published a book of anti-racist football poetry to 'celebrate cultural diversity in world cup year'.

Against bigotry

Celtic Football Club began the year by organising an appeal from prominent Scottish churchmen, politicians and educationalists to 'Stop the Hate'. As part of their 'Bhoys against Bigotry' appeal Celtic declared the country could no longer accept sectarian bigotry which disfigured Scottish society. Celtic has already worked through Glasgow education department for one year to get children from five to fourteen in 100 schools to examine the nature of bigotry and find ways of working against it. And Celtic, originally set up in the last century to meet the needs of the Irish who were excluded from existing football clubs, is now very consciously trying to be equally sensitive to the needs of today's black players and supporters.

• The above information is from the CARF web site, which can be found at http://www.carf.demon.co.uk/

Racist soccer teams face ban

Government task force calls for local action to end discrimination against black and Asian players

Racist teams will be banned from council pitches under proposals presented to the Sports Minister, Tony Banks, by the Football Task Force yesterday.

The report, one of a series commissioned by the Government last July, found disturbing evidence that while racism at professional levels has diminished in recent years, the problem remains deep-rooted at local level.

The Football Task Force has heard evidence from supporters, players, administrators and officials since it was set up under the chairmanship of David Mellor in July 1997 and will produce a report on topics including commercialism, disabled access, ticketing and merchandising.

'The threat of racism is a powerful deterrent to black and Asian people playing organised football,' says the latest report,

By John Duncan, Sports Correspondent

unveiled yesterday at Lancaster Gate. 'It can have a detrimental effect on a player's performance and persuade some to give up the game altogether.'

Insiders say that task force members were shocked by evidence they heard in Leicester about the scale of racist abuse at park level, ranging from verbal abuse by players to violent attacks.

'The threat of racism is a powerful deterrent to black and Asian people playing organised football'

'The clubs concerned told the task force of hostile behaviour of a racist character directed towards young players from opposing players, parents on the sidelines and in one case the referee,' says the report. 'Formal complaints have been made to the relevant county football associations but no action had been taken against the clubs or the individuals concerned.'

Leicester city council offers a good example of the problem faced by those trying to eliminate racism at local level. While the council organises one of the best ethnic soccer programmes in the country, the Leicester Asian Sports Initiative, the parks department says that it is unaware that there has ever been a problem of racism on its pitches and has not had any reports of incidents in the past two years, a statistic that does not accord with the experience of local black and Asian footballers.

The task force recommendation is based on the Hounslow Initiative which brought together clubs, leagues and county FAs to sign anti-racist declarations which appear at all council pitches.

Council officers have taken an active interest in racism on council pitches and, say locals, this has helped encourage more black youths into the game at park level. Similar schemes are now being operated in Liverpool, Sheffield, Watford, and Lewisham and Greenwich in south London.

The report also urges referees to adopt a 'zero tolerance' approach to racist behaviour, making racist abuse an automatic sending-off offence. The FA was asked to ensure that there was some black representation at higher administrative levels – there are none on the FA council, the governing body in England. Many black footballers complain that county FAs are similarly un-representative.

The Government immediately accepted the task force proposal to end the 'nonsense' that police are able to act against racist chanting by more than one person but abuse by an individual is not specifically illegal.

The Home Secretary, Jack Straw, said the law would be changed 'at the earliest possible opportunity'.

'The report has come at the right time,' said Robbie Earle, the Wimbledon footballer. 'Racism is still a serious problem and there is no place for it in the modern game. A lot of time and effort has gone into this far-reaching report which hopefully will set the standards for players and supporters.'

© *The Guardian*
March, 1998

Black footballers in Britain

Information from the Sir Norman Chester Centre for Football Research

The late 1980s and the 1990s – a 'new era'?

The 1980s saw a tremendous increase in the number of black players playing both for non-league part-time clubs and in the Football League itself. Indeed, a number of today's stars, such as Arsenal's Ian Wright, were first spotted playing non-league football. By the end of the decade, clubs which had no black players on their books were now very much in the minority. Although overt racism inside football clubs was beginning to decline, on the terraces, it still remained a problem. Also, black supporters continued to be a rarity at stadia across the country, even in areas where there is a substantial local black population. These two negative aspects were, during the seventies and for much of the eighties, consistently overlooked by football clubs, the game's authorities and also by the British Government.

By the late 1980s, a number of high profile clubs with little previous history of signing black players made significant moves into the transfer market. At Liverpool, John Barnes was signed for a fee of nearly £1 million from Watford, while at Leeds United, Rod and Ray Wallace were captured from Southampton. Viv Anderson and Paul Ince moved from London's Arsenal and West Ham, respectively, to Manchester United

whilst in Scotland, Mark Walters left Aston Villa to join Glasgow Rangers, a team idolised by a largely far-right causes (See, Murray, 1984). The Glasgow club banned some season ticket holders following racist abuse aimed at Walters.

Perhaps partially as a result of these high profile signings, overt racism on the terraces of football grounds began to decline. The success of local black players at Arsenal for example, has served to attract more black fans to that club's matches and to counter racism among local fans. At Liverpool, the signings of John Barnes, Mark Walters, Michael Thomas, David James and Phil Babb have not only led to a reduction in overt racism among the club's fans, but have encouraged a small number of black and Asian supporters to the club's home games. Finally, at Leeds United, where the problem of racism

had long been a feature of a vocal minority of home support, the signings of black players and the launch of an anti-racist campaign at the club involving supporters, the local Trades Council, the police and Leeds players, has gone some way towards curbing racist chanting and far-right activities in and around the Elland Road stadium (See Leeds TUC & AFA, 1987).

In addition to these local campaigns, the cause of 'kicking racism out of football' has been taken up on a national level, especially since the emergence of the post-Hillsborough period of reconstruction and modernisation of the professional game in Britain. New legislation introduced in 1991 which outlawed racist chanting at football matches gave the police new powers to arrest those fans who persisted in racist chanting. The work of a number of organisations, including the Football Supporters' Association, the Professional Footballers' Association, the Commission for Racial Equality, the Football Trust and that of football fanzines has contributed in challenging both hooligan and racist behaviour at football stadia.

Today, it is estimated that around 300 of the 1900 football professionals in England and Wales are black. Racism has not been eradicated from the British game, of course, as evidenced by the continuing involvement in hooligan disturbances of right-wing groups. However, most clubs now have black professionals, and in the wake of recent anti-racism campaigns, the problem of racism at British football stadia is, at last, being confronted. Black players now face the challenge of qualifying as managers and coaches in the game. Opposition here, in an institutionalised sense, still seems quite strong, with some established chairmen, managers and coaches questioning the coaching and managerial capabilities of black footballers. Black players have now largely established themselves as players in England; how long before they are routinely accepted on the management and coaching side?

Asians can't play football?

As British players, mainly from African Caribbean backgrounds, have gradually overcome racist opposition to their place in the British game, so attention has recently shifted to the lack of Asian players in the footballing profession. Currently (February 1995), no professional club in Britain has a professional player of Asian origin in their squad. Even in cities such as Blackburn, Bradford, Glasgow, Leicester and London, where there are large British Asian populations, there has been no Asian breakthrough. Why should this be the case?

Firstly, it will take time for Asian players to break into the professional ranks. Also, the cultural distinctiveness of the Asian community may be a factor. Cricket, not football, is the favoured national sport, for example, in India and Pakistan, though few British Asian cricketers have made it into the professional ranks of that sport in Britain either! Certainly, British Asians play football in large numbers (See Westwood, 1993; Fleming, 1993). As far as locally organised football is concerned, Asians play in considerably large numbers. A Manchester University study in 1991 found that a higher proportion of the Bengali community in Britain played football (60%) than any other, including white (47%), and that 36% of the Indian community and 43% of Pakistanis

played the sport compared with 26% of Africans and 34% of people of Caribbean origin. There are an estimated 300 teams across Britain playing in leagues organised by local Asian communities, set up mainly in response to the non-acceptance of Asian youths into white or mixed teams (Brown, 1995, p15). However, Asian players who have ambitions for a career in the professional game complain of their 'marginalisation'. For example, in 1994, a three-day tournament in Birmingham involving Asian teams drew over 5,000 spectators, yet there were no scouts from either Football League or FA Premier League clubs present (Brown, 1995, p16). So, are Asian youngsters in Britain just not good enough? Or, are other factors at work?

A new project (Bains and Patel, 1994) challenges the view that Asian footballers do not have what it takes to survive as professional footballers in the 1990s. This project aims to persuade clubs that they should be doing more to get Asians involved and will examine a new set of racial stereotypes faced by Asian players: that they are too small; undisciplined; culturally unwilling to 'integrate'; not committed to the game and so on. The project will 'monitor' clubs and their attitude towards Asian youngsters, and it will also ask Asian youth players about their ambitions to become professional players. Staff at some clubs acknowledge that the selection system they use in choosing

young players discriminates against Asians 'because they have not been regarded as likely pros' (Quoted in Brown, 1995, p15). Finally, the project aims to establish a 'Centre of Excellence' for young Asian footballers in England to better their prospects of making the grade. Who knows? In a few years we may well have a football captain of England whose roots lie in the Indian subcontinent.

References and further reading

Bains, J., Patel, R. (1994), *Asians Can't Play Football!*, Midland Asian Sports Forum

Brown, M. (1995) 'Asian Games' in *When Saturday Comes*, February pp. 14-17

Cashmore, E. (1982), *Black Sportsmen*, Routledge

Commission for Racial Equality, PFA, The Football Trust (1994). *'Let's Kick Racism out of Football'*

Fleming, S. (1992), 'Sport and South Asian Male Youth', PhD Thesis, Brighton University

Highfields Oral History Group (1994), *Highfields Rangers: an Oral History*, Leicester City Council

Hill, D. (1989), *Out of His Skin: the John Barnes phenomenon*, Faber

Leeds TUC and AFA (1987), *Terror on the Terraces*

Longmore, A. (1988), 'Black Revolution' in *Football Today*, November pp. 6-7

Murray, B. (1984), *The Old Firm: Sectarianism, Sport and Society in Scotland*, John Donald

Vasili, P. (1994), The History of Black Footballers in Britain (unpublished paper)

Walvin, J. (1986), *Football and the Decline of Britain*, Macmillan

Westwood, S. (1990), 'Racism, black masculinity and the politics of space' in Hearn, J. and Morgan, D. (eds), (1990), *Men, Masculinities and Social Theory*, Unwin and Hyman, pp. 55-71

Williams, J. (1992), 'Lick my boots...' *Racism in English football*, SNCCFR, Leicester University

Woolnough, B. (1983), *Black Magic, England's Black Footballers*, London

© Sir Norman Chester Centre for Football Research

Furd way forward

It's taken a long time for black soccer players to make it to the top. But the myth persists that Asians can't play. Chris Arnot finds Sheffield's Blades at the cutting edge of a campaign to kick racial stereotyping into touch

The English Football League season, apart from the promotion play-offs, officially ends on Sunday. But for a group of young Asian women in the Sharrow district of Sheffield, the action is only just beginning.

When Saturday comes, they'll be kicking off in the first of many summer matches. In a sports hall rather than on a playing field, mind you. They want to be well hidden from public view in order to preserve Muslim sensibilities.

When they're not enjoying a kick-about, they may occasionally revert to a more stereotyped pursuit – sewing. But in this case, they are likely to be making traditional shalwar kameez tunic and baggy trousers in the red, white and black-edged stripes of Sheffield United.

Mehrun Ahmed, a 32-year-old youth worker and mother of two football-crazy children, says: 'We want to get noticed when we go to matches.' There seems little doubt that they will be, whatever their costumes. When a dozen of them walked to United's Bramall Lane ground for the recent match against Manchester City, they received what Mehrun calls 'a few weird looks'.

But the women were, she admits, pleasantly surprised by the lack of evident hostility. 'We were quite nervous and we'd made careful plans about how we would cope with racist comments. But it didn't work out like that. It felt really good to walk with the rest of the crowd. For once in our lives, we felt part of the community instead of looking on from behind curtains.'

Mehrun is keenly involved with Football Unites, Racism Divides (Furd), sponsor of the women's matches and a project very much at the forefront of the game's fight against racial intolerance. It's not the biggest scheme of its kind – that honour goes to Charlton Athletic –

but, two years after its formation, it is widely regarded as one of the most effective.

Jas Bains, author of *Asians Can't Play Football*, had praised its effectiveness in promoting more involvement by the football club with the substantial ethnic minority population who live around the ground. 'They have done a tremendous amount of work in a short period,' he says in his evaluation.

'For some of the residents in the area it has been a question of shutting their doors and waiting until match day is over before they can return to some degree of normality. Part of that has been born out of experience and partly out of perceptions of the things football has been associated with in the past, but the project is beginning to have an impact in that respect.'

One notable success in changing perceptions has come from persuading Sheffield United to give away between 150 and 200 tickets through schools and youth clubs in poor areas with a high ethnic population – hence, the appearance of Mehrun and her friends at Bramall Lane. Price is a factor in deterring young fans from poor families, whatever their racial background. Some of those who benefit are white.

Entrance fees at Bramall Lane range from £10 to £16 and average attendances are around 17,000 in a ground capable of holding just over

30,000. So the club's give-away gesture is costing nothing, yet could have long-term commercial benefits – particularly if 'The Blades' reach the Premiership through this month's First Division promotion play-offs and demand for tickets increases.

Project co-ordinator Howard Holmes concedes that there is a certain amount of enlightened self-interest in the club's strategy. 'And why not?' he says. 'They've got a potential market on their doorstep which has been ignored.' What he would like to see now is more involvement from the players in anti-racist initiatives.

Holmes, 51, is a long-term season-ticket holder at Sheffield United. Like other members of the Blades Independent Fans' Association (Bifa), he was becoming increasingly embarrassed by racist chanting from a small minority at the Kop end of the ground. By the early 1990s, he was also acutely aware that there were fewer black faces on the pitch than there had been in the 1980s – and not many more in the stands. Bifa's success in helping to oust an unpopular club chairman had convinced him that supporters can make a difference.

In 1996, Furd became the first British project of its kind to attract money from the European Cities Fund. An exchange of information and tactics became possible with similar organisations across Europe, such as the Progetta Ultra in Italy. Already they were liaising with other agencies in Sheffield – not only the football club but the police, the Church and the city council's education and youth services.

Furd has an office in the stable block of an old house which once belonged to the Sitwells. On the walls are pictures of inspirational black players such as Manchester United striker Andy Cole, and Arthur Wharton, who played for the Blades in the mid-90s. The 1890s, that is.

Wharton was the world's first black professional footballer, a Ghanaian who could run the 100 yards in 10 seconds flat. His story has inspired a forthcoming Channel 4 screenplay by Phil Vasili and Irvine Welsh, and also provides a useful role model for Furd to take into schools and youth clubs. 'It helps when you can point out black players that have been around for more than 100 years,' says educational liaison officer Tom Collins.

Asian role models are more difficult to come by. At Furd's request, Sheffield United have appointed an Asian scout to scour the city for talent. A similar scheme will also be underway soon among Sheffield's Somali community. Meanwhile, Furd is also sponsoring some 40 black and Asian youngsters in their quest for FA coaching qualifications.

Youth worker Abid Rahim is one of them. He came to Sheffield from Karachi in 1966, when he was five. Both his father and uncle had played in Pakistan and young Abid soon latched on to United. During the 1970s, he says, it became increasingly difficult. 'I used to go to away matches and it sickened me the way my fellow supporters were shouting abuse out of the coach windows at black and Asian people in the street.'

The final straw came as he was queuing at a turnstile at Bramall Lane and found himself being jostled by white supporters, who told him: 'You don't belong here.' For a while, he felt safer at Hillsborough, home of Sheffield Wednesday, but such is the nature of football loyalty that he was inevitably drawn back to his beloved Blades.

'The racial thing has improved a lot,' he says. 'I still feel apprehensive, waiting for someone to make a comment, but at least the chanting seems to have died out.'

Not that he or Howard Holmes are counting their chickens yet. Both have supported Sheffield United long enough not to get overexcited by early promise.

On the Monday morning after they recently took 10 Asians to Bramall Lane for a strife-free Saturday afternoon, they saw an advertising hoarding nearby on which had been scrawled 'Wogs out'.

© The Guardian
April, 1998

Football unites, racism divides

Football Unites, Racism Divides believes that football, as the world's most popular game, can help to bring together people from different backgrounds to play, watch and enjoy the game, and to break down barriers created by ignorance or prejudice.

The project was started by a group of Sheffield United fans who were concerned about a number of incidents of racist abuse both in and around the stadium, which is situated in a community where about 44% of the local youth population is black or Asian.

Our aim is to ensure that everyone who plays or watches football can do so without fear of racial abuse and harassment, in either a verbal or a physical form, and to increase the participation of people from ethnic minorities in football, especially at Sheffield United, as either players, spectators or employees.

How do we aim to achieve this? We are involved in a range of initiatives – here are some of them:

Locally:

- Organise appropriate coaching sessions for both boys and girls

By Ruth Johnson

- Support ethnic minority men and women in becoming qualified football coaches
- Support local football teams with strong ethnic minority involvement
- Distribute concessionary match tickets in partnership with Sheffield United
- Work with Sheffield United to ensure it is seen as a secure and welcoming club
- Deliver football-based anti-racist education in schools, colleges and youth clubs

Nationally:

- Contribute to campaigns and discussions such as the national Kick It Out campaign and the government's Football Task Force report on eliminating racism
- Run a supporters' membership scheme for fans to show their support of our aims
- Run an anti-racist Resources and Information Centre dedicated to sport and related issues

- Publicise the story of Arthur Wharton, the world's first black professional footballer

Internationally:

- Run a website, including a discussion page
- Maintain links and exchange ideas with similar fan-based projects across Europe
- Help to enable teams to participate in international tournaments

For more information, advice or support, contact Football Unites, Racism Divides at: The Stables, Sharrow Lane, Sheffield S11 8AE. Tel/fax: 0114 2553156. E-mail: furd@furd.org Website: www.furd.org

The project is, or has been, supported by: The European Cities Anti-Racism Project, Regenerating Sheffield, Kick It Out, South Yorkshire Police Community Initiatives Programme, Sheffield Youth Service, Sheffield United Football Club, Commission for Racial Equality, Professional Footballers' Association, Churches' Commission for Racial Justice, the Home Office Community Relations Unit, and Sheffield TEC.

© Football Unites, Racism Divides (Furd)

ADDITIONAL RESOURCES

You might like to contact the following organisations for further information. Due to the increasing cost of postage, many organisations cannot respond to enquiries unless they receive a stamped, addressed envelope.

Anne Frank Educational Trust (AFETUK)
PO Box 11880
London, N6 4LN
Tel: 0181 340 9077
Fax: 0181 340 9088
E-mail: afet@afet.org.uk
To promote the message of education against discrimination in any form.

Campaign Against Racism and Facism (CARF)
BM Box 8784
London, WC1N 3XX
Tel: 0171 837 1450

Campaign Against Racist Laws (CARL)
15 Kenton Avenue
Southall, UB1 3QF
Tel: 0181 571 1437
Fax: 0181 571 9723
Campaigns throughout the UK against the Immigration Act 1971, the Nationality Act 1981, the Primary Rule and the use of passport controls within the country. Produces publications.

Catholic Fund for Overseas Development- CAFOD
Romero Close
Stockwell Road
London, SW9 9TY
Tel: 0171 733 7900
Fax: 0171 274 9630
E-mail: hqcafod@cafod.org.uk
CAFOD is the official overseas development agency of the Catholic Church in England and Wales. CAFOD's aim is to promote human development and social justice. They publish useful factsheets and information packs on issues, including poverty and racism.

ChildLine
2nd Floor Royal Mail Building
Studd Street
London, N1 0QW
Tel: 0171 239 1000
Fax: 0171 239 1001

ChildLine is free, national helpline for children and young people in trouble or danger. Provides confidential phone counselling service for any child with any problem 24 hours a day. Produces publications. Children or young people can phone or write free of charge about problems of any kind to: ChildLine, Freepost 1111, London N1 0BR, Tel: Freephone 0800 1111

Commission for Racial Equality (CRE)
Elliot House
10-12 Allington Street
London, SW1E 5EH
Tel: 0171 828 7022
Fax: 0171 931 0429
E-mail: info@cre.gov.uk
The Commission for Racial Equality is working for racial equality for a just society, which gives everyone an equal chance to work, learn and live from discrimination and prejudice, and from a fear of racial harassment and violence. Produces a wide range of factsheets, books and other resources. Ask for their publications list.

Crime Concern
147-150 Victoria Road
Swindon, SN1 3BU
Tel: 01793 863500
Fax: 01793 514 654
To work with local partners to prevent crime and create safer communities.

Football Unites, Racism Divides (FURD)
The Stables, Sharrow Lane
Sheffield, S11 8AE
Tel: 0114 255 3156
Fax: 0114 255 3156
E-mail: furd@furd.org

Football Unites, Racism Divides is a community partnership project aiming to ensure that all people who play or watch football can do so without fear of racial abuse and harassment, in either a verbal or physical form.

Runnymede Trust
133 Aldersgate Street
London, EC1A 4JA
Tel: 0171 600 9666
Fax: 0171 600 8529
E-mail: runnymede@btinternet.com
The Runnymede Trust is an independent research and policy agency which addresses itself specifically to the development of a successful multi-ethnic society. Our aim is to provide policy analysis, information, research and advice and to promote the value of diversity in our communities.

Sir Norman Chester Centre for Football Research
Department of Sociology
University of Leicester
University Road
Leicester, LE1 7RH
Tel: 0116 252 2741
Fax: 0116 252 2746
E-mail: jt20@le.ac.uk

The Football Association
16 Lancaster Gate
London, W2 3LW
Tel: 0171 402 7151
Fax: 0171 402 0486

Transport and General Workers Union
16 Palace Street
London, SW1E 5JD
Tel: 0171 828 7788
Fax: 0171 963 4440
E-mail: tgwucc@tgwu.org.uk

Youth Against Racism in Europe
PO Box 858
London, E9 5HU
Tel: 0181 533 4533

INDEX

* * * * *

Commission for Racial Equality (CRE)

www.cre.gov.uk

Click on any item in the list of contents at the top left of the home page to go straight to a more detailed list of the topics you can reach under that heading. If you can't find the information you need, try clicking NAVIGATE. Here you will find a site map, an alphabetical index and a list of links to related web sites. A wide range of CRE factsheets are can be downloaded as PDF files.

Searchlight

http://www.s-light.demon.co.uk/searchlight

Searchlight is a non-sectarian organisation in political, ethnic and religious terms which aims to combat racism, neo-nazism, fascism and all forms of prejudice. Their site has a selection of past magazine editorials from their *Searchlight* magazine archive.

Campaign Against Racism and Facism

http://www.carf.demon.co.uk

CARF is an independent anti-racist on-line magazine, chronicling British and European resistance to racism. It is also a resource and information base for community-based campaigns, co-ordinating and servicing many grassroots anti-racist initiatives.

Black Information Link

http://www.blink.org.uk

Black Information Link is run by the 1990 Trust, a national Black organisation. The site includes sections on everything from art and culture, to the Stephen Lawrence campaign, and the environment.

Britkid

http://www.britkid.org

This is a web site about race, racism, and life – as seen though the eyes of the Britkids. There is an easy-to-use guide to the web site that will help you locate any specific issues you might be interested in: black people and the police, music, racism in sport, marriage and relationships, prejudice and racism generally, immigration, prejudice and jobs, harassment, words and names, and racist jokes.

Institute of Race Relations

http://www.homebeats.co.uk

Have a look at their on-line Resources Section which covers: racism in the police and the criminal justice system, racial violence, racism and education, racism and fascism around Europe, third world and globalisation, refugees and asylum-seekers, racism and sport, general information about racism and black Britain.

ACKNOWLEDGEMENTS

The publisher is grateful for permission to reproduce the following material.

While every care has been taken to trace and acknowledge copyright, the publisher tenders its apology for any accidental infringement or where copyright has proved untraceable. The publisher would be pleased to come to a suitable arrangement in any such case with the rightful owner.

Chapter One: Tackling Racism

Racial attacks and harassment, © The 1990 Trust/Blink, *What is racism?*, © Commission for Racial Equality (CRE), 1997, *Racial discrimination defined*, © GREC, *Racist attacks and harassment*, © Britkid, *Public attitudes about race*, © Britkid, *Tackling racism*, © ChildLine, *You have rights against racism*, © Commission for Racial Equality (CRE), *Children and racism*, © ChildLine, January 1998, *Britain's ethnic mix*, © Policy Studies Institute, *An anti-racist charter for the new millennium*, © The 1990 Trust, *Don't shut your eyes*, © Commission for Racial Equality (CRE), *Regions of residence*, © Owen, D (1992-1995) 1991 Census Statistical Papers Paper 1-9, Centre for Research in Ethnic Relations, University of Warwick/CRE, *EU set to accept anti-racism law*, © The Guardian, March 1998, *Percentage in each ethnic group who had suffered different types of crime*, © British Crime Survey 1994, ONS 1996, *Stopped 60 times, never arrested*, First published in The Independent, September 1998, *Stop, search . . . and arrest*, © Crown Copyright, *Let us tackle racism together urges Jack Straw*, © Crown copyright is reproduced with the permission of the Controller of Her Majesty's Stationery Office.

Chapter Two: Racism at Work

Racial discrimination in employment, © Crown copyright is reproduced with the permission of the Controller of Her Majesty's Stationery Office, *Unemployment rates by ethnic groups in the Inner London area*, © Central London Economic Assessment, Focus Central London TEC, 1998,

Equality for all, © Transport and General Workers Union (TGWU), *Blue-chip world shuts the door on ethnic minorities*, © The Independent, January 1998, *Union equality*, © The 1990 Trust/Blink, *Staff fight to cure racism in the NHS*, © The Independent, October 1998, *Race relations*, © The Guardian/ICM, *Military 'must wage war' on racism*, © The Guardian, November 1998, *New plan to end racial harassment in the NHS*, © Crown copyright is reproduced with the permission of the Controller of Her Majesty's Stationery Office.

Chapter Three: Racism in Football

What's it all about?, © Kick It Out!, *Racism in football*, © Haringey Youth Online, *Andy Cole talks exclusively to Kick It Out!*, © Andy Cole Enterprises Ltd, *Attitudes to racial chanting by age*, © Pinto, T., Drew, D. and Minhas, N. 1997 Sheffield Divided or United? A study of 'Race' and Football. Sheffield Hallam University: The Survey and Statistical Research Centre/Football Unites – Racism Divides (FURD), *Anti-racism and football*, © Sir Norman Chester Centre for Football Research, *FA launch biggest footy racism crackdown*, © Caribbean Times, April 1998, *Percentage of non-white fans*, © 1997 Premier League Fan Survey, *Soccer's hidden racism: blowing the whistle*, © Campaign Against Racism and Facism (CARF), *Racist soccer teams face ban*, © The Guardian, March 1998, *Black footballers in Britain*, © Sir Norman Chester Centre for Football Research, *Furd way forward*, © The Guardian, April 1998, *Football unites, racism divides*, © Football Unites – Racism Divides (FURD).

Photographs and illustrations:

Pages 1, 6, 8, 11, 17, 21, 23, 26, 27, 33, 35: Simon Kneebone, pages 7, 25: Pumpkin House.

Craig Donnellan
Cambridge
April, 1999